Black Perspectives in Social Work

Black Perspectives in Social Work

Bandana Ahmad

Publisher: Jo Campling

In association with the Race Equality Unit
National Institute for Social Work (NISW)

Venture Press

Published by Venture Press
16 Kent Street
Birmingham B5 6RD

First published 1990
Reprinted 1992
Reprinted 1993
Reprinted 1994
Reprinted 1996
Reprinted 1999

Cover design Western Arts
Design and Production by Saxon Publishing Consultants Limited
Typeset in 10/11 Baskerville by TecSet Limited

Printed and bound in Malta by Interprint Limited

ISBN 0-900102-780

FOR MY GRANDCHILDREN
EMIL, RYAN, ADAM and SUSHMITA

Let them grow up in a multi-ethnic Britain with self-esteem and self-pride.

Contents

Acknowledgements

In 1983 I was one of the three Black women delegates to NALGO's annual conference. We were travelling together by train to our destination. My thoughts were preoccupied with a particular Black family, as I left after visiting the family for the station. The family's experience, like many other Black families, with the social services was fraught with social work incompetence and insensitivity. I was angry, I was hurt and I exploded soon after I was with my co-travellers. As my two Black sisters listened to my anger and hurt, sympathetically and supportively, they confronted me as well. One of them challenged my pain and frustration and stated – "your anger and hurt are not going to help the Black family – what are you going to do about it?" The other sister provoked me even further, "You should write a book – I know you are going to write a book one day." After seven years of that prediction made by Jasminder Stockbridge, I am particularly pleased to live upto her expectation.

This book could not have been written without the enriching experiences I have had with many Black families and Black professionals. They have been my source of strength, my guide for anti-racist social work. I have learnt much from them and continue to do so.

I could not have finished this book without the encouragement and support of my three children – Asif, Naeema and Naseema and collegues – Ratna, Arshi and Janette. There were times when I felt immense pressure to fit in my writing time amidst my never ending duties of 'directing' and managing the newly established Race Equality Unit and keeping up with my social and family responsibilities. Both my family and colleagues came to my rescue, creating time and space for me to get on with the book.

My special thanks to Jo Campling for making the publication of this book possible.

Foreword

When approached to write the preface to Bandana Ahmad's book, I was deeply moved by the honour of being asked to comment on the work of a black woman whose commitment to anti-racist practice was widely known. I was also hesitant about what contribution I as a white person could make to the evaluation of something written from a black perspective. Now, having read the book, I am more confident about my answer.

The first thing to say about *A Black Perspective in Social Work* is that it is highly relevant to both black people and white people. Taking the view that both black and white people can ultimately practice in non-racist ways, it addresses the different learning tasks that black people and white people have to undertake to reach non-racist standards in their work. Relying heavily on analysing examples of practice, the book considers case materials involving work done with black people by white social workers and demonstrates step by step the inappropriateness of the intervention which took place. As these cases were then passed on to black social workers, we are shown by direct comparison, the different ways in which black practitioners worked on the issues to provide a more user-centered, sensitive service. The question of what constitutes good practice with black people is handled in concrete terms. Black practitioners are made aware of the impact that practising from a black perspective can have on their work. White practitioners are given specific guidance, including checklists on points they must cover if black people are not to be damaged by insensitive and racist practice. The message that racist practice is invariably bad practice is continually made visible. The book is, therefore, written very much from a practitioner's point of view, addressing complex issues of practice in a clear, well-structured and well-thought out manner.

Addressing the issue of racism in social work, *A Black Perspective in Social Work* is timely. It joins a growing body of literature written by black people from a black perspective and provides documentary testimony to both the appalling practice white social workers have inflicted on black people and the ways forward which are indicated by a black perspective. Moreover, I found Bandana Ahmad's book optimistic as well as practical. I did not emerge from reading it feeling that I was doomed to being a product of my biology. I could indeed learn to practice in ways that were in keeping with a black perspective. And although I personally would have liked more connections being made between the eradication of institutional racism and improvements in one's personal practice, particularly in the final chapter dealing with the impact of 'race relations' and welfare legislation on black people, I end on this optimistic note. I hope that we can change both ourselves and the world in which we live to foster each individual person's welfare regardless of their racial or ethnic background and that we can bolster our commitment to carrying on the struggle to make this society a more congenial place. That is a major theme in Bandana Ahmad's book and one which I hope will motivate us all.

Lena Dominelli

Professor of Social Administration

Sheffield University

Setting the Scene

Recognition and acknowledgement of the different experiences and needs of Black and Minority Ethinic families, living in Britain, have been a periodical phenomenon in social work practice in the past two decades. In general, the manifestations of somewhat adhoc recognition and acknowledgement have been mostly confined, either to the debates on whether social work policies and practices have fully realised its obligations to Britain's Black and Minority Ethnic residents as part of 'Social Work Consumers', or to the denial of social work mistreating Black and Minority Ethnic families. What is common in both these debates and denials is a factor, which clearly demonstrates that there is some concern, anxiety and paranoia in relation to social work practice with Black and Minority Ethnic families. What is also an emerging factor is that, even if there is a will to make social work effectively applicable to Black and Minority Ethnic communities, often, in the absence of appropriate guidance, the transference of will into action faces difficulties. Consequently, social work recognition and acknowledgement of racial inequality in social work practice do not necessarily lead to equitable social work response and outcome, which in turn perpetuates racism in social work. This book makes an appeal to this social work will, which is struggling to transfer its will into action. In so doing, the book aims –

1. To establish a practical framework of good social work practice with Black and Minority Ethnic families.

2. To promote coherent and consistent development of ethnically sensitive social work approach and practice.

3. To equip practitioners with some usable tools in order to enhance their personal knowledge, skills and tasks for working with people from diverse backgrounds.

4. To encourage a continuous learning process that can be creative and have changing impacts on social work policies and practices.

In pursuing these four aims, this book invites both Black and White social workers to face squarely equal and empowering social work practice for and with Black and Minority Ethnic families. For White social workers, the book makes positive criticisms of those aspects of social work practice, that are influenced by white values, assumptions and perceptions, resulting in some appalling and distressing practices. Each criticism is analysed both from an 'user perspective' and a 'Black professional perspective', followed by an exploration of exciting possibilities for change – change in perception, change in social work methods and approaches.

In the main, the alternative methods and different approaches that are mentioned, stem from the knowledge base of Black professional experience and expertise, gleaned from examples of good practice initiated by Black workers. That is not to suggest that White workers have no contribution to make in social work with Black families. On the contrary, there are many references in all chapters about white academics and practitioners. There are examples of cross-cultural working in a mode of 'Black and White Alliance'. Most importantly, the book acknowledges the progression made by anti-racist White workers and perceives them as a valuable resource for change (Chapter 3).

For Black workers, this book aspires to push them further towards accreditation and validation of their own knowledge and experience, away from internalised denial of their own experience and acceptance of white domain in social work. If social work today with Black families is enigmatic due to its concern, anxiety and paranoia, as I mentioned before, then it is also troubled with the pain and frustration of Black workers, struggling to make social work responsive to Black families. It would be arrogant and presumptuous on my part to suggest that this book can do away with troubled pain and frustration. Rather, this book makes a humble but confident submission to the continuing and growing pain and frustration of Black workers (and anti-racist White workers), and seeks to demonstrate ways in which to fulfil social work duties and responsibilities to our Black families in need of services. No one should place the entire burden of making social work just and empowering on Black practitioners alone. Anti-racist social work must be a concern and aspiration for all. However, Black professionals have a crucial role in leading and guiding anti-oppressive social work intervention. Demonstration of how Black professionals can co-work with White practitioners and play a leading and guiding role, are featured in each chapter and case studies.

The choice of this terminology 'Black' in this book has been used to describe people mainly from South Asian, African and Caribbean backgrounds and other visible minorities in Britain. It is not the intention of the author to lumber all minority ethnic communities in an all inclusive term of 'Black' and depict these different and diverse communities as a homogeneous group. Rather, the term 'Black' is used to reinstate a growing sentiment of Britain's minority ethnic populations, who, in rejecting various classifications and categorisations imposed on them by White institutions, have crossed their geographical and cultural boundaries to consolidate their struggle against racism and oppression and unify under the banner of being 'Black'. This consolidation and unification has not been at the cost of losing ethnic identity and pride. The expression of being 'Black' has not been in contradiction with cultural diversity and ethnic differences. On the contrary, for many minority ethnic people, it has been a source of unified strength and solidarity, opening up more opportunities for celebrating and affirming ethnic identity.[1]

This book is written from a Black perspective. It is often asked what is a Black perspective. Interestingly enough, the same question is hardly ever, if at all, directed towards White academics, writing books and articles on Black people, or for that matter on any other issues. There is not an expectation of them to define White perspective. Yet, they must have a perspective which relates to them being White. I suggest that, White writers have not had to define White perspective, as 'White' is accepted as the 'norm'. Definition of Black perspective needs to address this anomaly first. Black writers need to refrain from any demands made on them to produce a neat definition of Black perspective. For Black perspective is much more than a string of words. It is more of a statement against 'White norms'; it is an expression of assertion that cannot be bound by a semantic definition. The factors that prescribe a Black perspective have a long history of subjugation and subordination. The circumstances that shape a Black perspective stem from the experience of racism and powerlessness, both past and present. The motivation that energises a Black perspective is rooted to the principle of racial equality and justice. The articulation that voices a Black perspective is part of a process that is committed to replacing the white distortion of Black reality with Black writings of Black experience.

Within the overall framework of good social work practice for Black families, the content of this book is placed in the context of the basic principle of care, including some of the main principles of social work and professional ethos and values. The principle and practice issues are addressed across social work settings, services and client groups. References to specific client groups are made only when it is necessary or appropriate.

Chapter one looks at the identification and assessment of Black client's needs. It lists main ingredients that are common in shaping the assessment pattern of Black clients giving six examples of case studies. Each case study is analysed and evaluated followed by suggestions of eclectic social work assessment of Black family's needs.

Racism and oppressive social work practices are in conflict with the 'caring' notion of social work profession. It is impossible to be a caring practitioner and be racist or oppressive at the same time, however unintentionally. Good intention on its own is not going to equip social workers to eradicate pathological and negative assessment of Black families. In chapter one, as social work assessment of Black families has been criticised and challenged, exploration of different ways in which anti-racist assessment can be made has aimed to establish a positive framework for assessment; a framework that can withstand criticism and challenge, a framework that can maximise opportunities for appropriate assessment of Black families.

Chapter one ends with a twenty-two point check-list. Any action or practice oriented approach has its risks. Apart from obviating from the conceptual understanding and awareness of how institutional and personal racism permeates all areas of social work knowledge and practice, there are other risks that merit warning. It is essential that readers, in particular White readers, do not follow the practical suggestions and checklists mechanically. Just simply running through a checklist or practice list, without continuous analysis and evaluation of the quality of social work and its outcome is running towards dangerous pitfalls.

Chapter two focuses on the concept of empowerment and its implications for social work practice in Black communities. The concept is contextualised in the two main aspects of social work practice – 'social welfare' and 'social control' and how racism has taken its tolls in these two aspects. It also examines some of the power dynamics that 'professionalises' social work practice against the interest of Black clients and quotes nine examples to illustrate disempowering effects of social work practice on Black clients and empowering options for social work practice. In advocating for empowerment of Black clients, the chapter calls for a 'Radical social work approach' and explores its potentials for advancing anti-racist social work ideology and ethos, social work resource and service, social work practice and social work monitoring.

In social work, there is a tendency to keep social work with Black families outside the mainstream framework of social work theory and practice. Perception and assumption that perpetuate this tendency usually stem from a notion that 'special' needs of Black families are so alien that they can not relate to the mainstream social work. Although it is a fact that the mainstream social work policies and practices are fundamentally eurocentric, it is also a truism that social work needs to get rid of its eurocentricism from its mainstream structures to become anti-racist. How can it be possible to rid social work from eurocentricism without anti-racist social work becoming part of mainstream social work? Furthermore, there are some empowering aspects in mainstream social work theories and practices. Social work with Black families can benefit from making use of these empowering aspects. To this end, chapter two addresses the concept of 'Anti-Racist Social Work' within the mainstream theoretical and practice framework in its section on 'Turning the key of empowerment in social work approach'. It identifies examples of good practice in Task-Centred, Unitary and Group work approaches and makes selective references to empowering features of these approaches. Community social Work approach is not specifically mentioned in this section, this approach is imbued in all chapters. Chapter three is about 'Resources for change'. It builds on the previous two chapters and makes further links with six specific sources of change for racial equality in social work practice.

Chapter four illustrates the implications of Race Relations Act 1976 for social work practice and makes references to some other legislative framework, in particular, Children Act 1989. All legislation has its drawbacks as well as advantages. No legislation alone can make social workers anti-racist. Much depends on how they interpret the laws or even abuse them to reinforce racism. Much also depends on how legislations are used as a tool to tackle racism in social work. It is in this context that this chapter includes specific sections of Acts, which provide opportunities for furthering anti-racist practices.

Reference

1. B. Ahmad – Self-definition and black solidarity – *Social Work Today* 11.5.1989.

Chapter 1
Identification and Assessment of Needs

Advocacy for client's participation in joint assessment with the professionals and partnership in making decisions, keeping the client informed about procedures and decisions, etc., are increasingly becoming popular and desirable for social work practice. In some local authorities social services departments (SSD) and voluntary agencies, such advocacy has gone beyond debates and discussions and has been structured through the policy of 'Open File' system. I begin this chapter with a particular SSD in the process of implementing its open file policy with a view to promoting clients' control over assessment of needs and decisions taken by the authority about their lives.

The work force of this SSD in general and their main unions were in full support of the departmental policy of open file, client's participation in case conferences and access to information and records etc. If there was some professional anxiety and concern about the implications of the new way of working with the clients, it was not perceived as being insurmountable against the strong belief in principle and practical support provided in terms of planning for consultancy, training and implementation of programme in phases. However, problems started once the work force, in particular the front line practitioners like social workers, day care workers and their supervisors, all White, began to look at their practices in relation to Black client groups. As they found it extremely difficult to change the way they identified the needs of their clients, they found it equally impossible to provide access to records and files to their Black clients. The expressed reasons mainly were –

– they (Black clients) do not understand how assessments are recorded and what for,
– we (professionals) have invited them before to discuss these issues but they do not want to come,
– they will not co-operate or agree with the necessary course of action,
– they will not like our assessments and be aggressive,
– we may not have made proper assessments due to lack of cultural awareness,
– we realise that in the past some of the assessments were influenced by prejudice and stereotype for which we can not be expected to be responsible,
– we need training on 'special needs' of Black clients before we can

implement 'open file' policy and practice.
– we lack necessary skills to deal with 'Black and White conflict' inherent in our work with Black clients and inevitable in sharing informations related to assessments and action, etc., etc.

The above expressions demonstrate certain common factors. They are as follows –

– No attempt to analyse the cause factors of the difficulties in carrying out the policy for Black clients as opposed to White clients.
– If there were some anxieties in relation to White clients, differences between those anxieties and worries about Black clients were not identified.
– In general, the White work force defined the needs of their Black clients as being 'special', instead of acknowledging the DIFFERENCES.
– Consequently there was a notion that Black clients' 'special needs' can only be effectively catered for by 'special' provision, which was outside the general or mainstream social work policy and practice.
– The responses were symptomatic and negative whether in terms of pathological perception of Black clients or deskilling evaluation of professional practice.
– Both explicit and implicit in the responses was the usual equation of Black clients with 'PROBLEMS', which fails to focus on professional performance and measure its quality and outcome.
– Most importantly, the risks of discriminatory practices against the Black clients were increased. The environment that had positive energy and encouragement of desired and shared social work policy and principle, could neither be wholeheartedly welcoming nor be beneficial to Black clients as opposed to White clients, who had more opportunities for exploring and sharing the pros and cons of 'open file' system, (for eg. a significant number of social workers and day-care workers made little or no effort to encourage Black clients to make use of the open system and some provided selective access to records and information.)

It is apposite to mention here that the above example is not a one-off experience of just on SSD. What the 'open file' policy did was to demonstrate a common pattern. A pattern that works against the interest of Black clients on the one hand and non-racist social work policies and practices on the other – whether by commission or omission. This section aims to list the main ingredients that shape the assessment pattern of Black clients.

"White social workers' pejorative assessment of black families and the reinforcement of racist stereotypes through their intervention are central to the '*social working*', i.e. social control, of black families and form the major avenues through which they '*clientise*' black people."[1]

It can be argued that, inspite of all the good intentions in the world, 'clientisation' of social services' users is unavoidable in most social work intervention and assessment. However, it can also be argued that 'clientisation' does not necessarily mean enforcement of 'social control' without positive interventions, ensuring welfare, self-control and self-development of clients. For Black people, the process of 'clientisation' operates within a depreciating model, inhibiting self-control and restricting welfare outcome. For Black clients, 'clientisation' is more related to enforced assessment and controlling intervention, than responding to the real needs of their families and communities.

Let me refer back to the responses of workers from the SSD with 'open file' policy and analyse some of the responses from the perspective of their Black clients.

- First, it was more likely than not that the 'reasons' expressed by the White workers could have been perceived as 'excuses' for not involving Black clients or denying their equal and rightful access to information.
- Second, Black clients could have challenged the credibility of the 'reasons', as according to their experience, preconceived assumptions were usually the basis for such reasoning, not the reality.
- Third, they could have pointed out that it was not a question of them not understanding assessment procedures, rather it was a question of not having the opportunities for acquiring knowledge about the procedures and participating in the process of assessment.
- Fourth, they could have justified their non-cooperation or disagreement or dislike or anger as essential pre-requisite of meaningful participation in bringing about the desired change in assessment practice, which in most instances do not relate to their real needs.
- Fifth, they could have assisted the social work profession in reviewing their methods of assessment and guided them away from subjective recording.
- And most importantly, they could have formed alliances with their White workers in tackling manifestations of racism, in particular, personal racism in assessment and recording, which is primarily at the root of cause factors.

"There is . . . a tendancy in Britain to use euphemism to obscure primary issues, or to use mechanisms through which secondary issues which result from primary ones are put forward as if they were the fundamental ones. In Britain, therefore, white racism is not highlighted as a primary issue; instead, courses for . . . social workers . . . if they give any attention to the issue of racism at all, concentrate on 'understanding them, their different cultures and lifestyles' in order to 'deal with them better'. There is less concentration, therefore, on racism as pervading phenomenon and more on the victims of racism as 'phenomenon for study' to improve 'understanding'. The net effect is that racism is reduced to 'racial disadvantage' and how to address that 'inherent' disadvantage. In so-doing 'the victims' become equated with 'the problems'."[2]

Without identifying the pervasive forces of racism in the identification and assessment of Black client' needs, social work profession may not only contribute to risk their credibility and accountability, but also jeopardise their own principles, as in the case of 'open file SSD'. So, what are their pervasive forces of racism that creeps into the identification and assessment processes?

The most damaging force that often shapes the framework of identification and assessment of Black clients' needs is White workers' pathological perception of 'Black family'; perception that has more commonalities with the racist belief of the superiority of White people, White values, White norms as opposed to the inferiority of Black people in general, than social theories and professional judgements. Examples of pathological perceptions of White social workers in relation to Black families have been cited by many sociologists and social work professionals, predominantly Black, in the past years, both in Britain and in the U.S. (Nobles,[3] Dubois,[4] Frazier,[5] Scanzoni,[6] Billingsley,[7] Hill,[8] Solomon,[9] Ahmed, Cheetham and Small,[10] Divine,[11] Ely and Denney[12].) The constant theme of nearly all the criticisms against the pathology of Black families has been, in main, a critical focus on 'Eurocentric' social work theory and practice, that devalues the strength of Black families by for example labelling them as 'disorganised', 'unstable', 'demoralised', 'apathetic', 'ignorant' etc., and denies the constraints of their reality determined by the past experiences (slavery and colonialism) and present predicaments (racial discrimination and harassment).

Let me illustrate how pathological framework operated in the following case studies hindering appropriate assessment and heading towards social work debacle.

Case study 1 – Mrs. B arrived in Britain from Sylhet with her four children to join her husband Mr. B in late 70's. Mr. B had been a resident in Britain for more than 20 years and had been an active member of a local mosque. Following the birth of the fifth child, Mrs. B was referred to a social services area office for depression and neglect of children. The assessment of the case by professionals ranging from health visitors to social workers demonstrated a pathological pattern – 'no English', 'culture shock', 'dominating husband', 'no idea about health care', 'no understanding of legal implications for children at risk', and so on. The case went through a few hands till such time as when it reached a 'radical' social worker, who was committed to join marches against Nationality and Immigration Acts and fight against male oppression. In less than three months' time, with the help and assistance of the 'radical' social worker, Mrs. B ended up in a women's refuge, only to find out that her three male children were not allowed in the refuge and even her two female children could be taken away from her. She attempted to commit suicide. The case was transferred to a Bangladeshi worker, who began to work with all members of the family, contacted those members of the community who had gained trust and confidence of Mr. and Mrs. B and made arrangements with an 'adopted aunt' to take care of the younger two children for a short period. The B family, slowly but steadily, began to regain their self-control over their lives and re-establish themselves as a family.

The list that follows gives a few pointers which could have improved the quality of assessment and hence enhanced caring practice, reducing the pain and strain of the B family.

1. Identification of the strengths of the B. family, in particular of Mrs. B.

For example, taking a positive account of the fact that Mrs. B nearly all her married life had managed without her husband and had the experience of bringing up her four children without the physical presence of their father. In addition, she must have had some stamina and skills to satisfy the rigorous immigration requirements and overcome the anxiety of travelling to Britain – thousands of miles away from Sylhet. Once here, she could have had a supportive structure in her community either through her husband's involvement in the local mosque and/or through her and her children's contact with other Sylheti families.

2. Understanding some of the constraints of the B. family imposed by the professionals.

If the reason for recording Mr. B's behaviour as being 'dominant' was part of identifying and assessing Mrs. B's and her childrens' needs, then it could have been quite misleading to make this judgement based on the simple fact that Mr. B did 'all the talking'. There could have been many other issues which could have left Mr. B with no other option but to do 'all the talking'. For example:

(a) it was more probable than not that the social worker (and other professionals involved with the family) did not speak the language (sylheti) of Mrs. B. It is apposite to mention here that nearly always, social workers (and other) professionals tend to place the responsibility of communication through language on the client, rather than on themselves. I am yet to see an assessment recording that acknowledges the absence of professional linguistic skills, hindering the quality of assessment. However, I have seen innumerable reports and comments on 'Asian' clients' problem of 'speaking no English' and recommendations for 'English language classes' for non-English speaking clients. It is regrettable that only a handful of social workers, who are committed to fulfilling their caring duties, are beginning to learn the language of their clients instead of expecting their non-English speaking clients to learn English and increasing the burden of their clients, who by social work definition are the most vulnerable members of our communities.

(b) Without the appropriate linguistic skills and effective interpretation service, the professionals used Mr. B in assisting them obtaining information. Otherwise they could not have made any assessments – good or bad.

(c) Since Mrs. B could not speak English and her husband could, he had little choice but to do 'all the talking' to satisfy and comply with the professional intervention. Furthermore, Mr. B was probably a valuable resource for the social work profession, which was bound to be dismissed on the basis of negative judgement made against him.

(d) On the other hand, if Mr. B's domineering behaviour was a cause for concern in protecting the welfare of Mrs. B and her child, then, instead of providing an opportunity to Mrs. B to express her needs without the influence of her dominant husband, at least during the assessment process, the professionals involved, made Mrs. B even more vulnerable by putting her in a predicament, where she found her domineering husband speaking on her behalf, resulting in having no control over her situation. Thus she could have been a victim of double oppression, whether in terms of marital relationship or professional intervention. It is a fact that the combination of institutional powers and dominant family forces forms a formidable alliance, exposing Mrs. B and her likes to further exploitation, endangering their and their children's welfare and protection.

3. Sensitivity and consideration of cultural expectations.

The arrangement of removing Mrs. B to a women's refuge could not have been more unprofessional and insensitive. That is not to say that the provision of refuge should not be considered. Many Mrs. Bs do often need such a provision for various reasons, ranging from the need to get some relief in a vantage point to making the first step in liberating themselves from family oppression. However, when consideration of refuge provision is made, careful thoughts and preparation are required before any action is taken in the following main areas:

(a) Exploration of all possible supportive resources, in particular, community resources prior to making arrangements for refuge.

(b) Comparison of the cultural and ideological framework of the refuge, in relation to residents like Mrs. B, who may not only disagree with for example 'anti-male' type organisation, but may also find it extremely distressing to comply with some imposed regulations such as parting with their male children or any other children.

(c) Supporting structure and the environment of the refuge that are conducive to the social and practical needs of women like Mrs. B, without which they can become even more isolated and/or be subjects of racial harassment from White residents of refuge.

(d) Information about the nature and purpose of refuge provision, including its credibility, accountability and reputation to women like Mrs. B and the members of their communities prior to any moving arrangements.

(e) Practice of ensuring client's options to choose from, of which consideration of moving away from the family or the community may be one and if chosen by the client, it is based on an informed decision without the influence of social work values of 'individual liberation'.

Let me explain it further within the context of traditional social work, which is based on the discipline of casework with heavy psychoanalytical orientation. "Fundamental to the casework model of social work practice is the western ideology of 'individualism', which perceives the individual as an entity and encourages that individual to supercede all social constraints by 'liberating the self' and 'securing individual rights'."[13] In this process, usually the 'problem' of the individual receives such exclusive attention that it tends to overlook other external and internal constraints of the individual. In doing so, the 'problem' of the individual is personalised by the social orker to the extent of perceiving the indivdual as 'the problem' and internalised by the client to the extent of losing any confidence of 'solving the problem'. The role of the social worker then is providing 'treatment' to 'cure' the problem of the client and the client is expected to perform 'tasks'. "Thus the client is at the receiving end of professional control, leading to an unequal exchange which perpetuates the ever increasing dependency of the client on the one hand and never decreasing control of the professional on the other."[14] In relation to Black women, application of the above model of social work has other implications. The major implications are manifestations of professional prejudice, that perceives these women as poor victims of their families and communities, that believes that the culture of Black families and communities oppress women, who are incapable of freeing themselves from oppression. It is hardly surprising then that in most instances, White social workers, in particular White women social workers, take on the responsibility of 'liberating these minority women' within their social work role.

I would like to point out that the above reference to the provision of women's refuge is applicable to other areas of supportive provisions, such as 'clients' groups', 'mothers and toddlers groups', 'women's groups' etc., which are often recommended to women like Mrs. B. These recommendations are justified, provided they take on board the issues raised so far. Evidence suggests that many women like Mrs. B have experienced tremendous pressure for joining such groups and stress of unease and unwelcome after joining such groups, only to leave within a short time with much sense of guilt for 'displeasing' professionals on the one hand, and increased sense of failure and decreased self-esteem on the other.

It is crucial that the social work profession recognises that even the most well intentional attempt of alleviating isolation or facilitating socialisation of Black clients, through group work or other supportive measures, that benefit White clients, may end up with adverse effects on Black clients, if the environment has some, if not all, the characteristics of power relationship between White and Black people in Britain. It is imperative that social work profession acknowledges the fact that the power dynamics between White and Black people in the British society, which determine their status in a hierarchical framework of the White Collective in the position of power and Black communities at receiving end of racial discrimination and harassment, impinge on

White and Black clients as well. As clients of social services both White and Black clients may have a common identity, but their racial identity may structure their relationship from the dominant position of the White society, its interest, views and values, norms and customs. In other words, Black clients may have little or no power in forming an equal relationship with White clients, let alone countering negative myths, stereotypes and assumptions of White clients. For it is a fact that Black clients may share some common problems of poor White clients, but they do so in much more acute form. Comparatively they are disproportionately worse off than their White counterparts. It is necessary then to understand why in the past years Black communities have begun to develop and establish their own autonomous physically distinctive organisations, that are expressions of their aspirations and expectations, that are demonstrations of self-definition of their own experiences, that are actions for fulfilling their duties and responsibilities of their communities. To ignore these unique community initiatives is to remain ignorant about valuable community resources, which social work profession can ill afford.

4. Positive use of family and community resources

The situation of the B family changed considerably for better following the intervention of the Bangladeshi worker. There is a danger to conclude that the ethnic match of the client and worker was the only determinant factor. To suggest this is to imply that the Bangladeshi worker had no skills other than belonging to the same ethnic group of the client and having the necessary cultural knowledge or language. Cultural understanding and knowledge of language have great benefits. However, these skills alone do not make a social worker. It is the ability to apply the skills through effective approach that makes social work credible. Mrs. B and her family benefitted from the way the Bangladeshi worker approached their difficulties and the worker's approach was significantly different to that of previous workers. While previous workers ignored the possible sources of support and assistance within Mrs. B's family and her community, her fellow worker explored the possibilities and succeeded in making positive use of family and community resources. This meant working with all members of the B family, on their own and as a family, sharing and exchanging information, counselling, contacting members of the community without breeching confidentiality or losing trust and confidence of the family, carefully planning and evaluating each step at the pace of the B family, owning up any mistakes made during the process and so on.

Use of community resources is not totally alien to social work practice. Indeed, in the past six years, the concept of, for example, Community Social Work has slowly gained access to social work scene. Recently, advocacy for community social work has been on the increase. However, this advocacy has not been without inexpedience. Even ardent advocates of community social work have found it laborious to clarify whether community social work approach can co-exist with 'orthodox social work', and if it does, when does the 'case work' end and community social work begin; is it another option that can be fitted in within the orthodox model, or is it a way of working that replaces case work and so on.

It is interesting to notice that while the debates and advocacies for community social work have been going on since the Barclay Report 1982, many Black professionals and nearly all Black organisations have been operating on community based model long before the theorisation of community social work model. While the social work profession has been more or less engrossed in identifying the implications of the Barclay Report, Black perspective in social work has predated the Barclay Report, as community social work has been right at the heart of the Black communities. One of the main reasons is that, contrary to the western philosophy of 'individualism', as mentioned before, most Black communities do not make unrealistic and distinct demarcations between the individual and the rest. Rather, self-development and self-achievements of an individual are appreciated against the support and assistance from the individual's family and community on the one hand and evaluated against the fulfillment of self-responsibility of the individual towards his or her family and community on the other. In other words, there is a reciprocal relationship, which cannot accommodate self-centred and selfish values thriving at the cost of the family and the community, nor can it endorse abdication from social duties and responsibilities, both in relation to the individual and his or her family and community. Consequently, when an individual experiences social problems that merit social work intervention, conscientious Black professionals have found it necessary to understand the problem of the individual within the roles and performances of not just the individual but the family and community network as well. In doing so they are able to assess the needs of the individual within the context of his or her family, community and society and respond to the needs accordingly. Thus the individual is not 'individualised' to the exclusion of other constraints and factors that may have either caused his or her problem or exacerbated the nature of the problem. As a result, instead of 'individualisation' of the problem, there is a joint ownership to the issues to be resolved.

Joint ownership means joint action that is more likely to alleviate self-helplessness of the isolated individual. More importantly, joint ownership and action, more often than not, lead to realistic understanding of those problems, which can not be resolved completely, as neither the individual nor his or her family or community have controls over the root cause of the problems. In such instances, all concerned (ie. professionals/individuals/families/communities) can begin to develop strategies for both tackling those aspects of problems outside their control and dealing with the source of control, whether in terms of campaign or collaborative action against those who have controlling power. For Black individuals, who become social work clients, racism with all its manifestations of harrassment, discrimination, poverty, oppression, poor quality of life opportunities, social stress etc., that are institutionalised and perpetuated through personal practices, most if not all social work related problems, have inherent elements beyond their capacity to resolve. As part of the Black community, Black professionals have also experienced racism which enables them to understand the debilitating effects racism can have have on their clients. It is hardly surprising then that conscious Black social workers have had little difficulties in adopting community social work model, which has more potential for assessing the needs of the clients against all the odds than personalised case work—which has more incentive for community based social work approach that can involve their communities than clientisation of the individuals.

It is perhaps regrettable that although for some time community social work has been perceived as a mode of progressive social work, it has neither recognised nor acknowledged the Black experience, for much could have been learnt from this experience. Instead, the evidence suggests that those Black professionals who have adopted community social work approach, have done so at the risk of being criticised and losing professional credibility. These criticisms have ranged from the accusations of 'over identification with the clients' to 'oppressing the individual with family and community expectations', and 'hindering the liberation of the individual'. Often such criticisms have been directed with threats of choosing between 'professionalism' (loyalty to social work agency) and 'advocacy' (campaigning with the clients).[15]

Case study 2 – Mrs. J, a Jamaican elder had been a resident of Britain since the mid 50s. Following the death of her husband in the late 70s and subsequent ill health, she gave up her council accommodation to live with her daughter, who found it difficult to take care of her mother living quite a distance away. The daughter lived in a small council flat with her three children and the father (unemployed) of the children. She worked in a hospital full time with irregular hours. Within a short time as various stress factors affected the family relationship to the point of near breakdown, Mrs. J's daughter sought help and assistance from social services department for care of her mother. She also made application to the housing department either for a bigger house for the whole family or for a small flat for her mother in the neighbourhood. According to the social services assessment form and social worker's report, Mrs. J's situation looked pretty good with comments like 'caring daughter and respectful grandchildren as in West Indian tradition', 'support of extended family' and so on. Stress and strain of the family were evaluated as a 'teething problem' with some passing remarks about the father, who 'needed some sorting out'. So Mrs. J's assessment could not justify the use of social services provision. However, her daughter was strongly advised to seek marital guidance. As far as the housing department was concerned, Mrs. J was not eligible for a council flat as she made herself intentionally homeless by giving up her previous council accommodation and the points given to the J family for a house implied that they could be on the waiting list for ever. Mrs. J rapidly became more ill with acute depression and finally gave in to her GP's advice to return to 'sunny' Jamaica. With great reservations her daughter and the rest of the family respected her decision and raised the money only to have to raise more money after three months to finance her return to Britain. This time Mrs. J came back to her family with not just poorer health but symptoms of mental disturbances. A few months later she was sectioned under the mental health act and diagnosed schizophrenic.

Mrs. J's case study is one of many that have tested the credibility and effectiveness of social work practice in relation to Black elders. Overall outcome depicts a 'non-caring' syndrome with discriminatory effects. How can it be otherwise? I will make reference to alternative methods of assessment within the framework of Black perspective. But before I do that let me mention a few points that require serious consideration.

"Social workers, doctors and councillors tend to assimilate generalisations about extended Asian families supporting its individual members, the matriarchal nature in the West Indies, and the role of the village elder in an African village. Few policy makers have close contact with ethnic minorities, and fewer still have bothered to ask the elderly in those communities how they see their life in Britain or what needs they have. The elderly in ethnic minorities in Britain are minorities within minorities." . . . [16] . . . "they have received less attention than they merit because of 'ageism', racism, ignorance, stereotyped thinking and because social policy does not aim to cater adequately for minorities."[17]

It seems quite evident that Mrs. J's case study (and many others) clearly substantiates the above statements. For example:

(a) Generalised and stereotyped thinking of Mrs. J's social worker (West Indian tradition) and GP (repatriation is best for depressed Black elderlies) led to inappropriate assessment of Mrs. J's real needs. What is particularly significant is that although on the surface the social worker's report seemed to be positive about Mrs. J's caring family, it failed to tap on the positive strengths of the family and ensure maintenance of Mrs. J's care in her family and community in Britain. Instead the report dismissed the J family's call for help by defining their reality based on generalised and stereotypical assumptions. Concommitant with the dismissal, the assessment and the inaction that followed, lost the opportunity of positively using community based resources. Social work profession seems to have too many lost opportunities in relation to its Black clients. Mrs. J and her likes may pay the price, but the ultimate cost is even greater for social work profession which claims to be the epistyle of warmth, humanism and care.

(b) Generalised and stereotyped thinking has other consequences as well. It often misdirects the assessment process to other areas of information that are irrelevant or not of specific importance to the problem. In Mrs. J's case study I mentioned the passing remark of the social worker about the father and professional advise for marital guidance to Mrs. J's daughter. If the passing remarks and subsequent advice were part of a comprehensive assessment that aimed to make a caring plan for Mrs. J, then the father 'needing sorting out' could have been one of other goals. But that was not so. There were no other social work plans or goals for Mrs. J. On the contrary, Mrs. J was left with a reminder that her daughter and the rest of the family were truly carrying the banner of culture and tradition of looking after their elders. Furthermore, it was not really Mrs J who had any real problems, rather it was her daughter who had problems with her male partner.

Overemphasis on Black men's sexism and oppressive behaviour towards women, to the exclusion of other social and welfare needs, is a manifestation of white perception, in particular white female perception of Black men. The perception is based on a belief that Black men, specifically of Afro-Caribbean origin are lazy and irresponsible; they exploit their women both sexually and financially. Such perception, when transferred to assessment of Black families without any appropriate reference, alongside its misguided effects, distorts the content of assessment with the inevitable outcome of deskilling and devaluing social work assessment. As evident in Mrs. J's case, her daughter's male partner became the primary social work target, not Mrs. J's needs.

(c) It could be argued that Mrs. J's social worker could do little as the assessment form dictated the criteria which Mrs. J did not fulfill. To a certain extent this could be true. Indeed most social services structures and mechanisms are designed to service white population. Hence, any criteria for eligibility and access to social services provision are more suitable to potential white clients than Black clients. It would be unjust to apportion the responsibility of formal requirements laid down by the management and policy makers to the general social work profession. However, there are hardly any criteria that are not open to professional obligations such as providing information about welfare rights and resources. In addition social work has never really ruled out possibilities of creative social work with vision and imagination. Mrs. J seemed to have missed out on all till she became 'schizophrenic'. What a way to be eligible! But was there not any other preventative measures for Mrs. J? There probably are no straightforward answers. But there are some straightforward questions. How did the social worker assess Mrs. J's eligibility? Did the assessment process seek information from other agencies such as medical report that could have supported Mrs. J's (and her daughter's) pleas for help? Was Mrs. J not eligible for any day care facilities? If she was, then was the reason why the social worker did not pursue this course due to the fact that all day care facilities were unsuitable for Mrs. J from Jamaican origin? If this was the case what prevented the social worker from recording this fact? Or was it the case that the social worker was not engaged at all in assessing Mrs. J's eligibility for social services' provision, but truly engaged in cultural stereotyping. Unfortunately, the probability is that the latter was the case as the others would have been easily detectable from records and reports.

It is against the background of painful experiences of Black families in need of personal social services that Black perspective in social work has emerged and established, however, unacknowledged and unaccepted in mainstream social work practice. This emergence has not been confined to Black social work (and other) profession only. Rather it has been rooted to the concern, initiatives and actions of their communities, determined to take control of their lives, committed to service members of their communities and resolute to protect their most vulnerable members. It has done its apprenticeship and learning from voluntary and community organisations, whether based in Black churches, temples, gurdwaras or community and resource centres. It has received its validation and accredation from Black communities, specially from those members of the communities who are or have been in need of personal social services. This is not to say that there have been no difficulties or ups and downs. Like any other community organisations, Black organisations are not immuned from certain drawbacks or pitfalls, which have direct effects on the credibility of Black perspective in caring profession. Like any other perspectives, Black perspective in social work has and will continue to have diverse and differing views. But what is unique about Black perspective is that it has a constant feature, that is community involvement and participation. This constant feature determines the way conscious Black social workers operate with their clients. Let me refer back to Mrs. J and give a brief account of how Black social work approach could have assessed her problem. The account that follows is not totally hypothetical. It is based on the empirical evidence of various examples of practice promoted by Black professionals in conjunction with their communities in many inner-cities of Britain.

Assessment of Mrs. J's needs –

1. Since Mrs. J's referral to the social services areá office came through her daughter (could have been Mrs. J on her own, GP, neighbour or somebody outside the family), there was an automatic access to the J family, which would have been identified as an advantage. For example, obtaining useful information from family members was more a possibility than probability. Information such as, Mrs. J's relationship with her daughter and rest of the family before she came to live with them and what were the stress factors that strained their relationships afterwards. Was it because Mrs. J needed much more attention and care than expected? Did the J family share the care of Mrs. J or was it entirely left to her daughter only? Did the J family resent Mrs. J for moving in to their small flat or blamed her daughter for her move? Did her daughter regret having her mother? Or was it due to cramped living, Mrs. J's daughter working irregular hours, father's unemployment etc., etc. Perhaps combination of all these factors and other contributed to near breakdown of the J family.

Recognition of these factors would not mean making negative assessment of the J family by labelling them as non-caring, unsupportive and cultural misfits. On the contrary, as the assessment would give full account of the difficulties experienced by Mrs. J and her family, it would also assess the implications of possible cultural factors, not cultural stereotype. If respect and care for elders are cultural factors, then the J family, in particular Mrs. J's daughter, could only seek external help when she could cope no longer. If, traditionally, Mrs. J was to be looked after by her family, then any attempt of lessening her family's caring duties and responsibiliies could generate her feeling of being rejected by her family, as it could increase her family's sense of guilt. Assessment of these cultural implications, in addition to all other caring needs of Mrs. J, could then begin to response to Mrs. J's situation appropriately.

2. There were other sources of valuable information that would be considered and discussed with Mrs. J. I have mentioned before about medical report. Although the main reason for obtaining medical report from the GP would be to gain information about Mrs. J's health, both physical and mental, it would not lead to assessing Mrs. J's physical and mental needs without critical evaluation of medical information. For example, GP's advice on repatriation to 'sunny Jamaica' would be questioned and attempts would be made to find out what kind of treatment or medical help Mrs. J had received for her depression. The roles of assessor and advocate would merge. Advocacy role would influence the social worker's assessment methods in seeking more information from other sources of expertise, in particular black expertise. Other sources of expertise would not be just medical profession. Sources would include Black or white colleagues with requisite knowledge and related experience, community organisations or members, Black pressure and campaign groups or Associations, Mrs. J's social and other contacts and so on. Implicit within this approach would be social work empowerment, as instead of being dismissed or unheard, the J family would get involved, however indirectly, in social work assessment; more importantly, in maintaining some control over the assessment methods, however gradually.

3. Assessment of Mrs. J and her family's housing need would not be totally left unchallenged to the procedures of Housing Department. Social work report would detail circumstances leading to Mrs. J giving up her previous council accomodation – circumstances other than poor health and physical distance from family, circumstances such as lack of personal social services provision for Black elders in the council, services provided by mainstream voluntary organisations designed for white elders. Social work report would also make reference to over representation of Black people in general, in poor housing, unemployment and other disadvantages caused by racial discrimination and harassment and assess Mrs. J's needs within the context of this reference. This would imply encountering housing department's defini-

tion of Mrs. J being intentionally homeless, putting pressure on the department for reconsidering points allocated and recommending short term provision. Social work assessment would also consider other housing resources like Housing Associations or Housing projects, preferably organised and run by Black members of the community. It is important to emphasise here that the challenging, critical and persevered nature of social work assessment does not necessarily follow access to and acquisition of desired resources. Shortage of housing is a reality, difficult if not impossible for any social work report to overcome. However, since social work assessment is about identifying and evaluating client's needs, it can hardly justify ignoring real needs of clients because needs can not be met due to lack of resources. Furthermore, inadequate resources, compounded by racism, has such debilitating effects on Black families in need of personal social services that their vulnerability is more intensified than white families with similar needs. Any assessment of Black clients, without taking note of these cumulative and differing effects, is bound to be incomplete, if not inaccurate.

4. In most instances, social work practice seems to operate in stages – referral followed by assessment and subsequent action or not. Only in extreme crisis situations, social work assessment and intervention overlap. In addition, in the hierarchy of crisis, preventative or creative social work practice receive least priority, both in terms of social work time and resources. Furthermore, social work intervention and prevention have not really had a corporate existance in social work policy and practice. While social work intervention has been the primary and central focus of generic social work, social work prevention has been assigned to a few and far in between 'community workers', outside the remit of social work practice. Consequently, few social workers are able to respond to crisis with tactical shift from reactive intervention to proactive prevention. As a result, social work practice in Britain has struggled with the rigidity of formal stages and juggled with crisis intervention and creative prevention.

Black perspective in social work has developed some useful strategies that can work around the rigidity of formal stages, cross the boundaries of generic social work and community work or community social work and incorporate preventative measures within social work intervention. For example, the strategies for Mrs. J would include some long and short term evaluation and planning during assessment. Long term evaluation and planning would aim to work as Change Agents from within social services institutions for establishing and promoting appropriate services for Black elders and resourcing community organisations. This would require clear understanding of how social services function, identifying key people that could influence change, forming alliance with sympathetic colleagues, in particular white colleagues and generating support network. But more importantly, consultative work with other Black professionals and expertise, liaison work with Black consumers, outreach work with Black communities and active participation in Black organisations would be vital for long term evaluation and planning. Mrs. J and her family would form part of a collective approach, engaged in assessing both their own needs and others in similar situation and evaluating and planning long term strategies for social work action. Short term evaluation and planning would focus on any possible immediate services for Mrs. J and her family. Following checklist in the form of a diagramme illustrates an example of short term evaluation and planning during assessment –

Diagram 1

Assessment of Mrs. J's Needs – Short Term Evaluation and Planning Checklist.

1 **Resources** Statutory/voluntary/communiy	
Aim	
Continuity of Mrs. J's care – some relief and breathing space for her and her family to work out better caring arrangements for the future.	
Explorations	
(a) Statutory	– Day and/or domicilliary care – Short term accomodation arrangement – Use of any special scheme/s and/or resources
(b) Voluntary	–Periodical relief of care – Volunteers and/or 'Befriending' programmes – Any practical assistance
(c) Community	– Local and/or national organisations/centres – Black Elders' groups and/or provision for black Elders – Family Friends and/or relations – Any other network

2

Welfare Services

Professional Advice and Counselling

Aims

1. To provide information on Mrs. J's welfare rights, provision for elders and possible choices and options available (or not) to Mrs. J and her family.

2. To share professional knowledge, criticism and appraisal of Mrs. J's experience within mainstream services.

3. To rechannel Mrs. J and her family's energy to those aspects of their lives that they can control or work on inspite of external constraints.

Actions

1. Presentation of relevant and understandable information and use of and co-working with other agencies more equipped and skilled in delivering welfare rights information as and when necessary.

2. Identification and clarification of Mrs. J's experience as a Black woman and as a Black elderly woman with statutory services against the overwhelming evidence of ill-informed advice and inadequate provision and possible consequences of her action based on this experience – for example returning to Jamaica.

3. Application of counselling skills in the above areas of action with particular focus on –
– awareness and understanding of external forces placing Mrs. J and her family in a predicament in order to develop skills to tackle the forces without internalising them as family problems.
– working through Mrs. J's feeling of rejection and her daughter's (and family) feeling of guilt and facilitating exchange of feelings.
– reinforcement of positive strengths of Mrs. J and her family.
– realistic expectation of Mrs. J's care arrangements and pragmatic approach in sharing her care.

3		
Support		
Family/Community/Professional		
Aim		
To reduce family stress and strain and maintain family strength.		
Facilitation		
(a)	Family	– Active participation and involvement of the J family in 1 and 2 (Empowerment). – Acknowledgement of individual members' limitations and complementing abilities.
(b)	Community	– Liaison work between the family and community initiatives. – Mrs. J's contacts with useful members of her community and any other supporting network.
(c)	Professional	– Gaining trust and confidence of Mrs. J and her family – Continuous discussion with and approval of Mrs. J in any decision planned or taken. – Continuous feedback to Mrs. J and as appropriate to her family. – Seeking advice from Mrs. J and her family on planning and practice issues.

Protection of a Black Child

"Nature brings the child into the world,
but society creates that child into a social being,
a corporate person.
It is the community which must
protect the child,
feed it,
bring it up and educate it.
Children are the buds of society,
and every birth is the arrival of spring,
when life shoots out
and the community thrives.
The birth of the child is therefore the concern
not only of the parents,
but of many . . ."
(From *African Religion and Philosophy*)

Gross over-representation of Black children received into care is a major concern that social work profession can no longer overlook.

Amidst the debates and campaigns, articles and reports on 'same race placement' vs 'transracial fostering', 'Black family for Black child' vs 'Cross-cultural adoption', 'Black identity' vs 'Human Bonding' and so on, the protection of the Black child is yet to overcome the outcome of poor social work assessment. What follows is a brief reference to a few Black child protection cases and an account of some common factors that usually guide social work assessment of Black children in need of protection. The account also aims to demonstrate a pattern which should shed light on improving the overall framework of assessment.

T was a mixed parentage child of a single white mother, who later on had a white partner and children from this relationship. All children were received into care and made wards of court following allegations of sexual and physical abuse against the white father. The children were placed with a white family, while search for a 'mixed parentage' family for T only (the authority had a policy of same-race placement) went on without much success. White foster parents and child psychologists argued against splitting up T from other siblings and social work assessment argued in favour of removing T from the white family in the interest of T. A suggestion of placing all children with a Black family was commented upon as being 'problematic'.

L was a Black child from Caribbean origin with severe mental and physical handicap awaiting adoption. Fostering arrangement with a Black family with possibilities of adoption was made with remarkable speed. The family returned their very first fostered child after much turmoil and with much distress, losing their confidence in fostering or adopting any child in future and risking judgements made against their ability to foster or adopt.

Assessment of M, a young girl of Asian background, concluded that she was sexually abused by her father. However, no immediate action was taken as the assessment made reference to 'cultural factors' and M's mother's fear of shame and community backlash. Following further reports of sexual abuse M was taken into care without further investigation and assessment, only to be returned to her family and the perpetrator of her abuse.

C's mother was mentally ill. Father cared for C, other children and mother. For financial reasons he was not able to give up his employment. All children including C suffered from poor health. Upon referral from Health Visitor, children were registered as children at risk and considered for reception into care as social work assessment was 'mother could not care for children'.

These four cases basically sum up what usually goes on in social work assessment of Black children in need of protection. Let me pick up some common factors that influenced and guided social work assessment of T, L, M and C.

1. All these children were not just victims of child abuse or being at risk, but they were also victims of ignorance, dilemma, unawareness, subjective judgement, insensitivity and prejudice of the social work

profession that had its toll on their assessment of protection needs. They were all at the receiving end of personal and institutional racism. Compare T with other siblings. Ask questions about how did the assessment of L's disability needs match other assessment criteria for L's placement needs apart from the family being Black. Make note of breech of child care proceedings in M's case, not forgetting traumatic consequences of assessment for M. Consider how fuller assessment of C could have widened the scope for alternatives other than reception into care.

2. All these children paid the price of social work assessment that was riddled with cultural paranoia, often misconceptualised as 'culturally sensitive'; and professional contradictions, often misinterpreted as professional convictions. T could either go to a 'mixed parentage' family and be separated from siblings or continue living with the white family and siblings against the conviction of 'same race placement'. Assessment against all children being placed with a black family raises several issues. What were the problems? Was the assessment based on cultural assumptions made about the suitability and ability of Black families providing care for White children? If it was, were the assumptions pathological? Or did the assessment show evidence of anti-black behaviour of white siblings? If it did, would it not have been in the interest of T to be either separated from white siblings or placed with them in a Black family who could help T to develop skills for tackling racist behaviour and other siblings in changing their racist prejudice?

L, with all the labels of 'hard to place' (Black and handicapped) and against all the cultural assumptions of Black families' reluctance to foster or adopt handicapped children had much less chances of finding another home that could balance the need of care and ethnic matching. For indeed L's assessment began and ended in finding a Black family, without detail assessment of necessary prearrangements such as professional advice and training, practical support and assistance and other important factors such as difficult survival experience of Black families requiring compensatory measures.

M was one of many, who had (and continue) to pay, one of the most highest prices of cultural assessment. In June 1989, in the wake of The Cleveland Inquiry, I wrote an article on 'Protecting Black children from abuse'. I quoted examples on how cultural paranoia and stereotype worked against the interest of Black children and mentioned three approaches prevalent in social work assessment. They were 'pathological approach', 'liberal approach' and 'safe approach'. Assessment of M managed to adopt all leaving her dislocated and more vulnerable than she probably was before social intervention. Pathological approach misinformed the assessment of cultural factors, such as acceptance of incest in M's culture and strict sanctions against M's family, particularly her mother, by M's community. Liberal approach distorted misinformation even further. It 'bent over backwards' to give precedence to the professional conviction of 'cultural sensitivity' at the risk of endangering M's protection, thus contradicting professional duty of protective intervention. The safe approach suited both pathological and liberal assessments at different stages. Culturally biased non-intervention was relatively safer than racist intervention; in other words 'no intervention means no racist intervention'. Interim removal of M was also safe compared to pressure of reports on M's abuse. Returning M back to further abuse was even safer to cover up the tracks of poor social work assessment.

Readers will recall that C's social work assessment more or less reinforced Health Visitor's assessment of mother's incapability. Although reference was made to father taking care of C and other children, the assessment completely bypassed his capability. Could it have been the case that C's mentally ill mother and physically stretched father needed some help and resources to overcome their difficulties in caring for C and other children? Or did the assessment make cultural assumptions about C's parents lacking knowledge of child and health care?

3. All these children were assessed against resource implications and assumptions made by the social work profession about resources for Black clients. In Mrs. J's case study, I commented on the correlation between social work assessment ignoring clients' real needs and availability of limited resources. In relation to Black clients, social workers often affix their assumptions about resources for Black people to their concern of restricted resources in general and make assessment of their Black clients, fitting them in, in line with their assumptions on resources. Usual assumptions on resources for Black children are –

(a) There are not enough numbers of Black foster or adoptive parents because Black families do not come forward to provide this service.

(b) Absence or limited numbers of Black Carers is due to the fact that they do not fulfil the requirements laid down by the authorities.

(c) In Black culture, concepts of fostering, adopting and caring outside the family network are not accepted.

(d) Social work time and resources are already so stretched to their limits that promotional work of finding Black families and Carers and additional work of providing support and assistance to newly found Black resources are not possible, however desirable.

Social work assessment needs to face up to the consequences of these assumptions and preempt them. The needs of aforementioned children and others like them can then be truly assessed. The following checklist aims to provide a framework for social work assessment of Black clients –

Checklist of Assessment of Needs of Black Clients.

1. Have you acknowledged the fact that all assessments of Black clients require recognition of racism and its effects whether covert or overt?

2. What steps have you taken to critically examine your values and perception of Black families?

3. How do you ensure that your assessment is not based on negative stereotypes of Black families?

4. Are you able to identify the root cause of your anxiety in the application of your assessment methods and skills without blaming Black clients?

5. How do you respond to Black clients challenging or criticising your assessment – constructively or defensively?

6. Are you confident to openly share your assessment with Black clients and their families?

7. Do you usually define the needs of Black clients or ensure your assessment is based on their experience and reality? How do you ensure your assessment is based on their experience and reality?

8. Do you assess strengths of Black clients, their families and communities as well as their weaknesses, problems and needs?

9. What have you done to ensure your assessment responds to *different* and specific needs of Black clients, *not* just 'special' needs?

10. Can your assessment make clear distinctions between clients' possible control of personal problems and external constraints beyond their control? What are the distinctions?

11. Is your assessment sensitive to cultural implications, expectations and aspirations? Make a list of cultural implications, expectations and aspirations.

12. Are you restricting your assessment because you think there are no resources, which justifies partial account of Black clients' needs?

13. Do you fit in Black clients' needs in your assessment or vice versa?

14. Have you made passing and/or irrelevant comments that may distort your assessment and misguide social work action?

15. Is your assessment capable of incorporating effective short and long term planning and evaluation?

16. Do you challenge and include critical assessment of racist procedures and practices of other institutions and professionals involved with Black clients you assess?

17. What steps have you taken to check whether your assessment is influenced by pathological, liberal or safe approach?

18. Are you fully aware of racist outcome your assessment may have on Black clients? Identify and list any possible outcomes that may be racist.

19. Do you actively seek and/or use advice and guidance from Black expertise?

20. Can your assessment advocate for change and race equality? How?

21. Can your assessment empower Black clients? How?

22. How do you evaluate your assessment of Black clients and outcome of your assessment on Black clients?

References

1. L. Dominelli (1988) – *Anti-Racist Social Work* – BASW – Macmillan 1988.
2. A. Ohri, B. Manning (Ed) – *Community Work and Racism* – Routledge & Kegan Paul 1982.
3. W. W. Nobles – Towards an empirical and theoritical framework for defining Black families – *Journals of Marriage and the Family* 40 – November (1978).
4. W. E. B. DuBois (1908) – *The Negro American Family* – Atlanta University Press – 1908.
5. E. F. Frazier – *The Negro Family in the United States* – University of Chicago Press – (1939).
6. R. Scanzoni – *The Black Family in Modern Society* – Allyn & Bacon (1971).
7. A. Billingsley – *Black families in White America* – Englewood Cliffs, NJ: Prentice-Hall (1968).
8. R. Hill – *The Strenth of Black Families* – New York: Emerson Hall (1972).
9. B. B. Solomon – *Black Empowerment – social work in oppressed communities* – Columbia University Press, New York (1976)
10. S. Ahmad, J. Cheetham, J. Small – *Social Work With Black Children and Their Families* – BAAF (1986).
11. D. Devine – Caribbean Times March 1983, *West Indian Digest October* (1986).
12. P. Elly & D. Denney – *Social Work in A Multi-Racial Society* – Gower (1987).
13. B. Ahmad – Community Social Work: Sharing the experience of ethnic groups – *Social Work Today* July (1988).
14. ibid.
15. ibid.
16. D. Johnson – The Quality Of Life Of The Elderly in Ethnic Minorities: *The Elders in Ethnic Minorities* – (Ed. F. Glendenning) – Beth Johnson Foundation Publications (1979).
17. C. Robinson – Foreword – *The Elders in Ethnic Minorities* – (Ed. F. Glendenning) – Beth Johnson Foundation Publications (1979).

Chapter 2
Empowerment

Black Rap

B.L.A.C.K.
Where do we stand in the world today?
get back! to the back of the queue
black and who are you?
black spot, black mark, black stain, black pain, black!
B.L.A.C.K.
where do we stand in the world of today?
get tripped, fall on your face
nigger boy ain't gonna run in my race
keep him on the floor an' kick him more and more
keep him on the floor an' kick him till him sore
black, black he's nigger and he's black
kick him in the head and kick him in the back black!
B.L.A.C.K.
where do we stand in the world of today?
well I've got no time subtlety
to give you what you want from me
I've tried and tried an' all have lied
I've tried again and again 'an again but all my tryin'
has been in vain an' now I'm their nigger boy nigger
boy yes I'm their nigger girl nigger girl
black!!
B.L.A.C.K.
where do we stand in the world today?
now that they know I'm black they ask me where I live
oh why do I feel that it's all take and no give
I say Mister Officer I'm in a children' home
they say hey step back you're on your own.

Lemn Sissay[1]

(from – *'Black and In Care' Conference Report October 1984)*

Where do Black clients, their families and their communities stand in the Caring Profession of social work in 1990? Evidence suggests, inspite of growing awareness of racial inequality in caring services, despite the increasing commitment to make social work profession ethnically sensitive and responsive to Black clients, there are still certain oppressive forces that disallow transference of racial awareness to recognising oppressive practices, that disaccord the rhetoric of commitment from social work action against racist procedures.

In 1980 I was one of the Ministry Advisers for Under Fives in a statutory agency. As I espoused a position of support and advocacy for the welfare of Black children and their families, I also engaged myself pushing for changes in agency procedures and practices, which, amongst many other strategies, required dialogue with the Head of the section, who was convinced that there was no need for any change. The Head also took much pride in pointing out that the Under Fives' section was way ahead in promoting racial equality than any other sections in the social services department, as indeed more than 80% of children receiving services were Black!

Since my encounter with evaluation of racial equality in social work, I have had many other similar encounters with social work managers and professionals, some of whom claimed even more. Their claim was expressed as deep concern about discriminating White children and their families, who, according to them were under-represented as consumers of their services! Some others went even further and clearly dismissed Anti-Racist policies and practices, as they had a long history of working with many Black clients. A critical examination of the Head's understanding of racial equality and similar claims favouring Black children and their families at the cost of White children and their families, dismissal of Anti-Racist policies and practices on the grounds of work history with many Black clients, reveals a major difficulty in measuring social work outcome on the one hand and clarifies some of the characteristics of oppressive forces in social work with Black communities on the other.

While social work has vacillated between helping clients and imposing statutory duties, it has strugled to cope with its conflicting roles of empower and control, often creating 'conditions of ambivalence'[2] and presenting moral and professional dilemmas. If, to a great extent, social work vulnerability is inevitable due to its 'problem' or 'crisis' type work, then added ambivalences and dilemmas make social work even more vulnerable, precipitating provisos for defending its credibility and accountability against any criticisms or challenges. One of the much used defending provisos is measuring social work competence in quantitative terms. In other words, numbers (personnel, hours, caseloads, clients) take precedence over the quality of social work in ameliorating 'problem' or 'crisis'. This has significant implications for social work in Black communities, where any challenge or pressure for change are perceived as attacks against social work profession and labelling it as being racist – much worse than being incompetent. So the number games become popular defending provisos, as if, the more the number of Black clients, the more the evidence for racial equality; and the less the number of Black clients, the less the need for changing policies and practices. Empowerment of Black clients and their families is tied up in this number game, as both their under-representation and over-representation are used as measuring devices for social work competence. Consequently, what remains unaccountable is the fact that the qualitative social work in Black communities is neither measured nor made credible in relation to Black communities.

Quantitative and qualitative impact of social work policies and practices in relation to Black communities can perhaps be best measured in the analysis of over-representation and under-representation of Black clients in social services and related agencies. Since the early seventies, Black individuals, whether from professional or community sectors, have been aware of their over-representation in the controlling aspects of personal social services as opposed to gross under-representation in the welfare aspects of these services. Initially this awareness was based on informations gathered through community network about the number of Black children in care and in probation and later on about Black people with mental illness. This awareness, apart from generating great concern, began to recognise social work control, inherent in these areas of social work procedures.

Recognition of social work control was not just based on information network and personal experiences of Black families whose children were taken into care. It was also based on evidence assembled by Black organisations. For example, in 1977 The Soul Kids Campaign[3] published its findings, which clearly substantiated concern for disproportionate number of Black children in care. The concern was even more intense as the facts also revealed that a large number of these children were very young, of mixed parentage (one parent white and one parent Black) and were likely to remain in care all their childhood. Following The Soul Kids Campaign, several other research studies and Reports CRE,[4] Home Affairs Committee Report,[5] Ousley,[6] Batta and Mawby,[7] Association of Black Social Workers and Allied Profession,[8] Black and In Care,[9] have continued to reconfirm over-representation of Black children in care. The trend still persists, particularly in most local authorities in inner-city areas. The trend also exists in other "enforcement" aspects of social work that are directly or indirectly related to the probation sector. In addition to the fact that Black juveniles (and young persons) outnumber their white counterparts in the Probation Service[10 and 11], more than half of these black juveniles seem to be subjected to Care orders as well.[12]

For some years over-representation of Black people in Mental Health services has been well observed and well established [13,14,15,16,17,18,19,20,21 and 22]. It is well acknowledged that Mental Health services are involved in social control and as such Mental Health professionals have power to enforce controlling functions, including the law. The correlation between over-representation of Black people in Mental Health scene and exposure to social control is not hard to identify. There is more. Mental Health services are not all about control and enforcement. Within the statutory and legal framework, there are many welfare type provisions available in Mental Health services, but Black people are under-represented in these welfare provisions, as above studies and others have shown. Burke (23), in challenging institutional racism in Mental Health services and expressing his concern about over-representation of Black patients in secure psychiatric units and selected psychiatric settings, stated, "Essentially the mental (social) control aspect of psychiatry is far more evident among Blacks than mental illness treatment and mental health promotion aspects which instead are predominant white concerns." Fernando[24] identified similarities between over-representations of Black people in prisons and in compulsory care in psychiatric institutes and concluded, ". . . psychiatry is involved in social control systems that keep black people 'in their place', i.e. within limits set by (white) society,".

If Black people were equally represented in the welfare aspects of caring services then their experience of being at the receiving end of social control would have been counter-balanced with the experience of being at the forefront of social justice. Unfortunately that is not the case, as most apparent in the ominous absence or negligible presence of Black people in welfare type personal social services, such as Counselling, Group Work, Information/advice/guidance (e.g. re-conciliation, conciliation, marriage guidance), services for Disabled, Respite Care, Support for Carers, Recreation/Leisure for disabled and mentally ill and above all services for Elders.

Under-representation of Black Elders in social services is no longer a mere assumption. Nor is it solely because Black Elders are ignorant about their rights and welfare services or they are reluctant to make use of services, as have been pointed out by many, periodically. That is not to say that Black Elders do not need information about their welfare rights and entitlement of personal social services. Indeed they do and should be informed by the caring profession as part of day to day practice. However, in order to fully understand the implications of welfare vs control for Black families, within the framework of social care, it is necessary to take account of some crucial factors and facts.

If under-representation of Black Elders in social services is mainly due to the fact that they 'rely on kinship ties', 'do not claim benefits', 'are not aware of state provision' etc., etc., then it can be argued that the same applies for their family members, including children. It can be further argued that since Black families lack knowledge and information about social services and other related agencies, they should have been under-represented in all sections of these agencies. But we have a different picture. Black people's lack of knowledge and information has not reduced the number of Black children in care, nor has it rendered few Black clients in mental health institutions. It seems then that the experience of Black communities, in general, is such that they are becoming well informed and knowledgable about the controlling aspects of social services, but not the welfare aspects. Why? Could it be because social services are more engaged in social work control over Black families than social welfare and services for Elderly people are welfare orientated? Should the social and other welfare services have involved themselves with Black Elders as they have done with Black children for example, Black people's experience of services received would have automatically enhanced their knowledge of services available for Elders and increased opportunities for obtaining information about pension scheme, home helps, sheltered or residential accommodations and any other benefits or entitlements. Regrettably, social services' involvement with Black Elders has not been as energetic as it has been with Black children. Fortunately, some social services are beginning to acknowledge their non-involvement in the past and some are acting on the findings of gross under-representation of Black Elders in their services for the Elderlies.

The following is a brief account of some of the findings that substantiate under-representation of Black Elders in social services.

Since the mid-seventies reports and studies, both at local and national level, have shown how most caring institutions have not really fulfilled their caring duties and obligations to Britain's Black Elders. (Abrams,[25] Anwar,[26] Bhalla & Blakemore,[27] Glendening,[28] Barker,[29] SCEMSC[30], Norman[31].) Most of these studies focus on 'Asian' and Afro-caribbean Elders. In relation to Chinese Elders "The research findings showed about 90 per cent of the Chinese old people interviewed had not received any help from social workers, home helps, community nurses or meals-on-wheels. Even in many cases where needs were apparent no help had been received."[32] Ely and Denny[33] found that it was usual ". . . to find a vey low take-up by black people (elders) of officially 'integrated' services. Pursuing a 'colour-blind' (same for all) policy may appear to be non-discriminatory but effectively excludes Black people from its provisions: an outcome that suggests 'passive racism'."

Roys,[34] in comparing Black children in care and Black Elders' care pointed out that ". . . Black consumers are under-represented as clients receiving the preventative and supportive elements of social services provision. . . Such under-representation of Black people in the supportive aspects of social services may help to explain over-representation in those aspects of social services activity which involve overt social control and institutionalization." He also argued that the 'invisibility' of Black Elders in social services and 'staggering' numbers of Black children in care of social services are a 'disturbing state of affairs', resulting in Black consumers entering a 'downward spiral' of statutory intervention and control. Unless and until the social work profession actively works against the debilitating forces of this downward spiral and stops Black people entering it, empowerment of Black clients may never be a possibility, let alone a reality. For, once entered, it is most difficult for the clients to get out of the vicious circle of downward spiral, as it is equally difficult for social workers to pull their clients out of the vicious circle of downward spiral. It is both in the interest of Black clients and social workers that empowerment can begin to replace 'social work enforcement' with 'social work enhancement', liberating social work profession from its oppressive roles and creating a social work climate where Black clients can take control over their lives.

Solomon[35] defined empowerment as a " . . . process whereby the social worker engages in a set of activities with the client or client system that aim to reduce the powerlessness that has been created by negative valuations based on membership in a stigmatized group. It involves identification of the power blocks that contribute to the problem as well as the development and implementation of specific strategies aimed at either the reduction of the effects from indirect power blocks or the reduction of the operations of direct power blocks." Since racism is one of the major powerful forces that blocks social work empowerment in relation to Black clients, it is necessary to establish a framework for non-racist social work practice. The section that follows is aimed at providing some practice guides for establishing personal (and institutional) framework for non-racist social work practice and promoting social work empowerment.

I will start with four specific skills suggested by Solomon as characteristics of non-racist social work practitioners –

First, 'the ability to perceive in any behaviour – other's or one's own – alternative explanations for that behaviour, particularly those alternatives which the self might most strongly reject as false'. In order to acquire this skill Solomon warned against easy temptation to 'seize that generalization which best fits' professional's 'predilections without adequate appraisal of the alternatives' and selective utilization of 'extremely limited and stereotypic set of generalization about black clients and their problems'.

Second, 'the ability to collect objectively through the senses those verbal and non-verbal cues which would help to single out of all possible alternatives the one that is most likely or most probable for a given client'. To this end she cautioned against holding on to preconceived notions (e.g. negative or stereotype beliefs) and risk the danger of 'closing off' the search for the most likely alternatives.

Third, 'the ability to feel warmth, genuine concern, and empathy for people regardless of their race, color, or ethnic background'. Feeling warmth, concern, empathy etc., are nothing new in social work practice. Acquisition and application of these skills are fundamental to social work encounter. However, social work encounter with Black clients often has difficulties in applying these fundamental skills. These difficulties may vary from personal prejudice against Black people in general to dislike or disapproval of behaviour or values of Black clients – or simple paranoia and mental block in dealing with Black clients. It is imperative that these difficulties are acknowledged by social workers as a first step 'in a process whereby the practitioner moves from self-awareness to self-control, i.e. the ability to control heretofore unconscious aspects of one's personality which have served as an obstacle to establishing warmth, genuine concern, and empathic relationships' with Black clients.

Fourth, the ability 'to confront the client when true feelings of warmth, genuine concern, and empathy . . . have been misinterpreted or distorted by the client.' There is evidence to suggest that often Black clients are denied the opportunities of receiving assistance and guidance from social workers because the workers, instead of working through the difficulties that may require confrontation at some stage, avoid the issues completely. Such avoidance is based on a belief that social work confrontation with Black clients can be misconstrued as being 'racist'. I will argue that avoiding appropriate and necessary social work confrontation is the same as social work inaction, and any social work inaction for Black clients is racist.

How can social workers acquire the skill of confrontation without being racist? Here are some pointers:

(a) Effective confrontation, particularly in a situation where the professional is White and the client is Black, requires social work confidence and competence.

(b) Social work confidence and competence in confronting Black clients can only be gained when social workers are continuously aware of their own perceptions and values that have racist connotations or may lead to racist outcomes.

(c) Continuous awareness of racist connotation and outcome stipulates an on going programme for self-evaluation. In other words, checking out what impact, specifically qualitative impact, self awareness has on practice.

(d) An essential requisite of an ongoing programme of self-evaluation is self-confrontation, i.e. confronting one's own approach and incentive for expressing warmth, concern and empathy that may be insensitive to the Black client's dignity and pride (e.g. patronising), or may not relate to the real problems of the Black client (e.g. concentrating on those aspects of the problem that least require expression of warmth, concern and empathy). Social work confrontation of social work profession precedes social work confrontation of Black clients, at least at the initial stage. At a later stage, when there is a confident and competent framework for non-racist confrontation, social work confrontation of Black clients and social work confrontation of social work profession can be simultaneous.

Identification of power blocks and removing them for enhancement of social work empowerment with Black clients, is closely related to identifying social work power and its implications for social work practice in Black communities. Hasenfeld[36] in demonstrating how the concept of power is usually neglected by most helping professions, identified four main sources of social work power. They are:

– "power of expertise which is derived from their (professionals) access to and command of specialised knowledge."

– "referent power or pursuation, which emanates from their interpersonal skills, particularly their ability to develop empathy, trust and rapport with the client".– "legitimate power which is an appeal to dominant cultural values and authoritative norms" and

– "power used by social workers, namely the resources and services" as members of organisations that control "critical resources", "the intake, processing, and termination of clients": that set out "departmental rules and regulations" and "professional norms and ethics"; that institutionalise norms and ethics as part of social work practice.

How do these sources of power have implications for social work empowerment with Black clients?

Case Study 7 – Ms. H was referred to a Black community Resource and Advice Centre by a social worker. The referral was made through a brief written note, stating Ms. H needed a place in the Women's Refuge run by the centre, which Ms. H handed over to one of the centre workers after a long and tired journey, minutes before the centre was due to be closed in early evening. Distressed and exhausted Ms. H was not in a state to provide information about why she was referred or how the social services department was involved with Ms. H. The centre worker decided to take Ms. H to the refuge and make immediate arrangements to make Ms. H as comfortable as possible and give some assurance without detail interrogations at this first contact. The assurance also made it clear that it would be necessary to obtain information and liaise with the social worker. As the centre worker engaged herself in obtaining information from Ms. H and liaising with the social worker, she co-worked with the warden of the refuge (day to day support/counselling etc.,) and another centre worker (practical arrangements such as clothes/money etc.).

Ms. H's male partner had committed incest with their 10 year old daughter who was in voluntary care. Father was in prison. Daughter resented Ms. H for informing the police about the incest (and incidents of physical violence to Ms. H), who according to her was 'jealous' of father 'loving' her more than her mother. Mother and daughter relationship broke down completely and as a last resort Ms. H agreed to place her daughter in social services' care.

At the same time Ms. H had to move out of her rented accomodation as conflicts with the landlord over arrears of payment was compounded by various other facts, such as, the rented accomodation was part of the whole house shared with the landlord and the family, wife of the landlord was distantly related to Ms. H's male partner and the comings and goings of the police, social worker, section 11 worker etc., proved too much for the children of the landlord.

Before long the centre worker realised that although according to the social worker's expectation her role was to provide refuge accomodation for Ms. H, she had to challenge this expectation and extend her role to influence social work practice both in relation to Ms. H and her daughter. The social worker responded to this challenge positively. A joint approach involved all main parties concerned, i.e. Ms. H, her daugher, the social worker and the centre worker – an approach that primarily aimed to empower Ms. H, so that she could begin to deal with her problem and restore her parenting role.

The process of empowerment had many components. The most important components were –

Sharing the Power of Expertise and Command of Specialised Knowledge

A pre-requisite of this sharing process was an acknowledgement of the social worker of those aspects of her expertise and professional knowledge that could not help Ms. H. For example, she evaluated her performance prior to sending Ms. H to the centre and identified how she used her social work power by concentrating on the formalities of sexual abuse and voluntary care without much considerations for supporting and advising Ms. H. What little considerations she had, she felt unable to follow them through actions, as she was convinced that she did not have a clue of where to begin with her Black client. She felt uncomfortable while making visits to Ms. H's home and threatened by the close presence of the landlord's family, which made her feel powerless. However she had the power of choosing the controlling functions and abdicating from other supportive actions. Her abdication was manifested in passing on these aspects of social work to the section 11 worker and later on to the centre worker.

Critical evaluation of this 'manifestation of abdication', which at a first glance looked like the social worker 'giving up' or 'sharing' power, began to look like quite the opposite. The social worker, even in her abdication, continued to use her power of expertise and command of social work knowledge to control both the section 11 and the centre worker and in turn Ms. H. How? Following indicators provide some answers.

First, the social worker did not really engage herself in sharing all information with Ms. H, section 11 and centre worker. Instead she informed them selectively. Selective information was based on pre-determined choice of what she wanted from them, particularly from the section 11 and centre worker, not what they could do for her.

Second, the social worker's approach in separating 'professional' issues (child abuse work) from 'cultural' issues (section 11 work) gave her an easy option to find comfort in her social work power and to conclude that she had dealt with both these issues, although the 'cultural' issues were passed on to others. In other words, partial involvements of the section 11 and centre worker (determined by selective information) were more for validating her social work approach than empowering Ms. H.

Third , the social worker established a hierarchical framework, her position being at the top and Ms. H at the bottom, with two 'cultural' workers, not so much in the middle, but more in the peripheral social work, dragged in the middle when needed to defuse encroachment of 'cultural' issues into the 'professional' issues.

Fourth, selective information, pre-determined expectation, partial involvement and hierarchical framework disempowered both the section 11 and centre workers, increasing social work control in their roles and severely restricting their ability to empower Ms. H. In this context, they were in the same position as Ms. H – without much control over their work.

Inherent in the social worker's evaluation of social work performance and identification of the above indicators was laying a foundation for sharing the power of expertise and command of specialist knowledge between Ms. H, the social and centre workers (section 11 worker had left the department). This was possible as both Ms. H and the centre worker were involved in the process of evaluation and identification and some ground rules for their involvement were jointly agreed upon by the three members. Agreed ground rules were in two main categories – (1) *what should not happen* and (2) *what should happen.*

(1) 'What should not happen'

(a) The social worker should not expect Ms. H and the centre worker to 'spoon feed' her.

(b) The social worker should not be on a 'guilt trip'.

(c) The social worker should not feel 'threatened' for being labelled as 'racist', when challenged by Ms. H and/or the centre worker.

(d) Ms. H and the centre worker should not use the social worker as a vehicle for transporting all their anger against racism or frustration against racial inequality.

(e) Ms. H and the centre worker should not dismiss the social worker's feeling of pain and disappointment that were inevitable in this process.

(f) The social worker should not ignore the feeling of oppression and distress that were part of Ms. H's and the centre worker's life experience.

(g) None should personalise comments or points made by members.

(2) 'What should happen'

(a) In relation to 'expertise and specialised knowledge', there should be an exchange framework which would require the social worker empowering Ms. H and the centre worker with information about social work methods and procedures; and Mrs. H and the centre worker guiding and directing the process of evaluation and identification with their knowledge of what social work expertise and specialisms were relevant or not to Ms. H and her daughter.

(b) Within this exchange framework, Ms. H and the centre worker should make positive criticisms about those aspects of social work expertise and specialisms that were irrelevant or detrimental to Ms. H and her daughter and the social worker should consider the implications of these criticisms for her practice – good social work practice.

(c) Implications for good social work practice should be the main focus throughout the process and the responsibility for maintaining the focus should be equally shared by all members.

(d) This sharing of responsibility should imply that during the process any member could challenge or confront deviation from the main focus.

(e) Challenges and confrontations should be substantiated and more importantly should be supported with possible alternative proposals.

(f) Possible alternative proposals should be discussed and debated with a view to reaching agreements.

(g) Once agreed, members should refer back to the exchange framework and implement their plan of action strengthened by each member's experience, expertise and command of specialist knowledge.

Developing Interpersonal Skills and Promoting Trust and Rapport

One of the direct outcomes of the sharing process established by Ms. H, the centre worker and the social worker was enhancing interpersonal skills of all three members that not only empowered Ms. H and the centre worker but the social worker as well. I will explain the empowerment of the social worker after Ms. H and the centre worker.

Empowerment of Ms. H

(a) In practical terms, evaluation of social work performance gave her some time and space to be free from social work intervention without worrying too much about her day to day needs met mainly by the refuge worker and her co-residents.

(b) Since Ms. H knew that temporary release from social work intervention would not result into social work termination, (the purpose of the release was to assist her more effectively) she was able to express her anxieties and communicate her concerns more openly, whether in relation to her situation or her experience with the statutory agencies. The centre worker's linguistic skills and cultural understanding were most crucial in assisting Ms. H in this process.

(c) Ms. H's increasing opportunities to communicate in her own terms meant that she was able to gain confidence in her communication skills and transfer these skills to take active part in interpersonal situations. For example, during the social work evaluation and planning, there were times when disagreements and difference of opinions between the social worker and centre worker reduced 'trust and rapport'. At these times, Ms. H's interpersonal skill of 'persuation' enabled the two workers to work through their disagreements and differences constructively. What was most significant in Ms. H's skill of 'persuation' was that she applied her other interpersonal skills (empathy, senstivity, mediation, reconciliation, negotiation etc.) in her persuation skill.

It is important that the readers make note of Ms. H's interpersonal skills, particularly her skill of empathy. The concept of empathy is hardly a new phenomenon in social work theory and practice. Indeed the ability to empathise is perceived as one of the key social work skills. However, this skill is usually promoted from the professional angle and directed towards the client. In other words, the client is the receiver of professional's empathy, not the other way round. This one way traffic of empathy can jeopardise empowerment of clients, if the clients' ability to empathise with the professionals is not recognised and appreciated.

(d) Recognition and appreciation of Ms. H's skill of empathy by the social worker and the centre worker had inherent empowering factors. In relation to the social worker, Ms. H's empathy developed due to her informed analysis of some of the limitations the social worker had in dealing with her situation. As she developed her skill of empathy, she used it to assist the social worker to get rid of some of the limitations with sensitive but firm approach. For example, although Ms. H was prepared to understand how the social worker, being white, could have overlooked cultural implications, she was not prepared to make continuous allowances for such omissions in future.

In relation to the centre worker, Ms. H based her skill of empathy on the shared experiences of being Black and her understanding of the difficulties the centre worker was facing in dealing with social services. This she did with strengths gained from her longer life experience than the centre worker on the one hand and easing the centre worker's distress through comforting gestures on the other. Combination of all these interactions meant that Ms. H was no longer the sole receptor of social work empathy. On the contrary, she became a valuable provider of client empathy as well, which enabled both the social worker and the centre worker to engage themselves in their empowering roles.

(e) For Ms. H, this reciprocal process of empowerment opened up opportunities for contributing to the 'promotion of trust and rapport' in social work approach. Furthermore, her partnership in this context proved to be a monitoring device for measuring the quality of 'trust and rapport', as the outcome of distrust and dissension, however covert, had direct effect on her and her daughter's lives.

Empowerment of the centre worker

(a) The centre worker's involvement in social work evaluation and critical appraisal of social work performance in relation to Ms. H required application of interpersonal skills in gaining access to social work power and securing professional acceptance of her 'command of specialised knowledge'.

(b) Consequently, her 'persuasive' skills, were more directed towards the social worker than Ms. H.

(c) Pre-requisites of 'persuasive' skills were continuous refinement of communication skills such as articulation, presentation of criticisms, adaptation of a challenging but non-threatening approach and realisation of balancing 'protesting' and 'proposing' skills.

(d) Inherent in the refinement of these communication skills was the self-empowering process of promoting confidence and competence.

(e) Self-confidence and competence enabled the centre worker to establish 'trust and rapport' with Ms. H and the social worker.

Empowerment of the social worker

During the process of social work evaluation and social work performance in Ms. H's case, it became quite inevitable at one stage that the social worker, inspite of having the power of 'social work expertise' and 'command of social work knowledge', felt thoroughly de-skilled in her interaction with Ms. H and the centre worker. As a result, she was unable to make use of her interpersonal skills which she frequently used with her white clients. Fortunately, her feeling of being 'de-skilled' did not persuade her to opt out of the sharing process that was jointly agreed and the ground rules that were jointly set out. Instead she began to use her 'persuasive' skills for 'self-persuasion' and apply her 'communication' skills with Ms. H and the centre worker as learning tools. The more she was able to rechannel her skills of 'persuasion' and 'communication' in this way, the more she was able to regain her social work confidence and professional credibility.

For example, as Ms. H and the centre worker guided and directed the identification processes of which aspects of social work expertise and specialisms were relevant to Ms. H or not, the social worker was more able to concentrate on the relevant aspects. This meant, she was able to use her time and enegry constructively instead of wasting them on irrelevant aspects. More importantly, this meant that she was able to make appropriate use of her 'expertise and specialised knowledge' and assist Ms. H and the centre worker. This also meant that she was able to seek assistance from the 'expertise and specialised knowledge' of Ms. H and the centre worker without feeling de-skilled. As she empowered Ms. H and the centre worker with her social work expertise and knowledge and received in return their help and support, she promoted her interpersonal skills in communicating without imposing social work control, demonstrating her empathy without being patronising and establishing trust and rapport without exploiting. Consequently, she was one of the main beneficiaries, as her interactions with Ms. H and the centre worker expanded the horizon of her social work expertise and knowledge and enhanced her interpersonal skills and she was empowered.

Power of Institutionalised Values and Rules and Professional Norms and Ethics

Social workers do not operate in a vacuum. They bring in their personal values that are influenced by their own socio-economic, educational and cultural experiences to their profession. If their personal values are based on the dominant cultural values and institutional norms, then it is more likely than not that they are socialised to the mainstream institutional values and norms with greater ease than those who belong to the minority cultural groups. It is also more probable than not that they are much more in tune with their organisational ethos and aims and objectives than their minority counterparts. In fact, they are the key members of their social services organisation, without whom the institution can neither operate nor achieve its goals. They are the main source of operational force, without which their institution can not deliver services and carry out its tasks. Above all, they are the primary task force of their organisation, without which it can not maintain its interest in controlling resources, setting up rules and regulations and standardising procedures. All these have great implications for institutionalising social work profession and social work power. The section that follows aims to identify some of these implications in general and make particular reference to Ms. H's case as appropriate.

There is a power relationship between social services decision makers and social services practitioners. It is a truism that the decision makers (management, politicians) have the ultimate power of controlling resources, establishing rules, regulations and procedures and most social workers are not necessarily involved in the decision making process. However that does not follow that social workers are mere robots. On the contrary, they have inherent power vested upon them as shapers and carriers of decisions, whether they are directly involved in the decision making process or not. Moreover, even though social workers may be bound by the decisions made from the top, the boundaries define how they can use their power. The definitions are based on mainstream ideology and ethos, which, as mentioned earlier on, are shared by the mainstream social workers to a large extent. Thus, there is a correlation between the decision making power and social work power, one supporting, endorsing and reinforcing the other. So social work practice not only reflects organisational principles and policies, but it also 'advances them'.[37] It is in this reflection and advancement of principles and policies that social work power is most active. Social workers then need to identify how their practice reflect and advance those principles and policies of their institution that are racist whether by design or default, that have racist outcome whether by omission or commission, that are discriminatory whether directly or indirectly, if they believe in the empowerment of the Black clients.

Ms. H's social worker was able to identify some of the aspects of her practice that reflected and advanced her organisation's principles and policies to the detriment of Ms. H. They were—

(a) Oppression—"The Philosophy of empowerment suggests to me a paradigm shift in the theory of social work practice, a move towards a practice. This construes clients as typically oppressed rather than disadvantaged. . ."[38] Portrayal of Black people as being 'disadvantaged' has been a constant pre-occupation of policy makers, researchers, reporters and practitioners. The list of 'disadvantages' has grown longer and longer—poverty, low incomes, unemployment, ill health, poor housing, low educational achievements, little or no command of English, lack of knowledge, generation conflicts, immigration stress and many more. As the list has grown longer, general focus has been on the symptoms of Black people being disadvantaged, not the causes and the causes are rooted to oppression.

"British society is saturated in oppression. They are based upon race, class, gender, age, disability and sexual orientation,"[39] For social workers, it is often an easier option to focus on the symptoms of oppression than on causes of oppression. It is so because, working on the symptoms of Black people's disadvantages, to the exclusion of tackling causes, means that the social workers can draw a parallel between Black people and disadvantages and conclude that 'disadvantaged Blacks' (there are distinct differences between 'disadvantaged Blacks' and disadvantages experienced by Black people) are not capable of being empowered. So they find little discomfort in exerting their power in 'helping disadvantaged Blacks' and boosting their caring ego.

Inclusion of tackling or even addressing Black client's oppression (causes of symptoms) is not comfortable for social workers as this requires acknowledgement of racism (one of the main causes) and dealing with it. Acknowledgement of racism shifts the focus from 'disadvantaged Blacks' to 'Black people being oppressed'. Dealing with racism shifts the focus from 'helping disadvantaged Blacks' to 'tackling oppressors' and redraws a parallel between Black people's oppression and oppressors, not between Black people and disadvantages per se. The parallel between Black people's oppression and oppressors brings the social workers much too close to the 'oppressor' category as part of the dominant society and members of the mainstream institutions. Engrossed in the 'welfare' and 'care' model of social work, most social workers find it extremely laborious to come to terms with their oppressive roles. However, the conversion from 'helping disadvantaged Blacks' to 'getting rid of oppressive roles' makes it equally troublesome for social workers not to own up to their capacity to proliferate oppressive causes of oppressed symptoms. The process of owning up their oppressive role forces them to acknowledge their personal racism and tackle it, however discomforting and distressing it may be. The usual syndrome of passing the buck of oppression to others and blaming institutions, managers, politicians etc., for racism becomes difficult. It becomes equally hard for them to dismiss the fact that racism does not exist as an external or 'out-of-focus' dimension in social work practice. It then brings to light why social work values, its professional norms and ethics need to be interrogated and scrutinised. Most importantly, it urges social work action that can 'shock' the social work system as opposed to gentle rock of social work empowerment. Crossing the hurdle of gentle rocking to systematic shocking is a must, if social workers wish to radicalise their social work power instead of liberalising their social work empowerment, as this is the first and foremost essential step of social work empowerment.

(b) Liberal vs Radical Social work Approach—"The rallying slogans of the 1960s and 1970s—'self-determination', 'community control' and 'power to the people', are but faint memories in the minds of many of today's community organisors. Community empowerment has become a non-issue. Yet community problems—housing, health care, employment, racism and the like—are worse than ever and the voice of the people has been undermined by years of baseless promises, liberal rhetoric and services that get at the surface but do not even touch the causes of oppression."[40]

There is a tendency in social work profession to disengage social work practice from political debates and political advocacy. Yet, social work in itself is 'undeniably political'.[41] This anomaly is usually couched in a liberal like social work approach, which may embrace the ideology of 'individual freedom', but need not concern itself with societal flaws that are fundamental barriers to individual freedom—barriers like sexism, racism and other oppressive 'isms'. A liberal social worker gets so involved in the so called 'individual freedom; that s/he tends to accommodate *all* individuals, irrespective of their socio-economic, educational or cultural backgrounds, in his/her pluralistic view of society. So the result is 'trying to please *everybody'*.

"The liberal then, is one who sees 'both sides' of the issue and shies away from 'extremism' in any form. He wants to change the heart of the racist without ceasing to be his friend; he wants progress without conflict. Therefore, when he sees blacks engaging in civil disobedience and demanding 'Freedom Now', he is disturbed. Black people know who the enemy is, and they are forcing the liberal to take sides. But the liberal wants to be a friend, that is, enjoy the rights and privileges pertaining to whiteness and also work for the 'Negro'. He wants to change without risk, victory without blood."[42]

In apportioning the blame for not tackling oppression to liberal social workers, who "have 'safety net' and 'enterprise zones'", Russell-Erlich and Rivera[43] questioned, "Why the liberal social worker establishment is still not sure of its position and strategies . . ." and stated that, "Perhaps it is because we still do not really want to be identified with the truly poor or jeopardise our positions by insisting that we pay attention to oppressed communities or retaining a commitment to fundamental social change". Liberal social work approach, in effect, is a safe approach. On the surface, it can make safe assumptions "that the interests of the client and the worker are compatible'', but can mask its ''importance of power in shaping worker-client relations''[44] . . . behind its bureaucratic structures, which provide ''a rather safe and secure context out of which the definition of professional and professional roles . . . can be clearly described,''[45] So, why shake the structures? Why lose 'earned right' to hold 'privileged status'? Why 'risk' management 'intimidation', 'nullification', 'isolation', 'defamation' or even 'expulsion'?

"Anti-racist social work is not a case of simply adding 'race' onto our considerations of a basically benign social work. What is required is the transformation of social work practice through the creation of social relations fostering race equality and justice. To move in this direction, social work has publicly to adopt a political stance against racism on cultural, institutional and personal levels within practice . . . and challenging a professionalism whose neutrality disguises support for the status quo. Professionalism will have to be redefined in terms of white practitioners taking sides against practices endorsing racial oppression, and transforming their work."[46] Radical social work approach provides a framework which can make this transformation possible. The framework exists – although usually avoided and underused. From time to time committed White social workers and conscious Black social workers have attempted to radicalise social work practice, but regrettably they have been and still are in the minority. Yet, the concept of social work empowerment is rapidly gaining popularity. I suggest that real social work empowerment, whether in relation to Black people or White people, depends on radical social work approach. The tenets of radical social work approach are summarised in the following checklist.

Checklist for a Radical Social Work Approach

This checklist is not a new invention nor is it a new formula. Rather it is based on various suggestions and recommendations advocated by many social work academics and practitioners over the years. Moreover, I do not present this checklist as a definitive answer to radical social work approach. It would cease to be radical if it was definitive, hence static. Radical social work is a dynamic and continuous process, which no amount of checklists can exhaust. However, a checklist that can provide a practical framework with limitless scopes for social workers to build on it and expand it further, has its usability. How the readers will do that will no doubt be reflected on the future relationships between social work professionals and Black communities; hopefully not social work control relationships but social work empowerment relationship. For this reason, the central theme of this checklist is Empowerment, as radical social work with Black communities is about social work empowerment.

The checklist is mainly aimed at practitioners. This is deliberate. As mentioned before, empirical evidence suggests that, for various reasons, personal and organisational, most practitioners, either remain indifferent or do not see themselves as a valuable source for social work change. They usually leave it to their managers and politicians or blame them for not achieving social work change. It is about time social workers face up to their responsibilities and take active part in freeing social work from oppressive practices.

The checklist is divided in four main headings – Empowerment as social work ideology and ethos, Empowerment as social work resource and services, Empowerment as social work practice and Empowerment as monitoring social work in Black communities.

1. Empowerment as social work ideology and ethos

(a) Acknowledgement of 'power' as a central element in social work practice.[47]

(b) Embracing 'empowerment' as social work domain and social workers as 'empowering agencies'.[48]

(c) Recognition of the effect of social work power compounded with racism (and other -isms) on Black families.

(d) Basing social work on a fundamental belief that the members of the Black communities are 'fellow citizens' with equal welfare rights and that social workers have a duty to make their 'citizenship' real.[49]

(e) Commitment to ensure that Black families have equal access to quality of social work services that does not reinforce 'social control' and 'surveillance', but facilitates 'prevention', 'rehabilitation'[50] and self-control.

(f) Alteration of the hierarchical power relationship between White workers and Black users (and workers) of services in a way that can neither render oppression invisible nor make it possible for social work 'experts' to substitute the 'voice' of the oppressed.[51]

(g) Counteracting myths of negative valuation of Black families[52] and moving on to a 'non pathologising understanding'[53] of Black families' problems and difficulties.

(h) Commitment to put empowerment of clients first, that subordinates material temptations such as job security, promotional opportunities and any other professional perks, that may call for not giving in to social work 'coping mechanisms such as capitulation, withdrawal, specialisation, or self-victimization.'[54]

2 Empowerment as social work resource and service

(a) Orientation of 'environment centred'[55] social work that is able to use service agencies as resources for the empowerment of Black clients.

(b) Sharing organisational power vested upon social workers as a resource for establishing partnership with Black clients in promoting Black clients' power resources and reducing organisational and professional dependancy of Black client.

(c) The above can be achieved by –

(i) recognising that social policy theories and social work practices are inseparable,[56] and exposing the connections between policy and practice.[57]

(ii) using service agencies as information resource (collating and disseminating) for increasing the knowledge and understanding of Black clients.

(iii) seeking critical comments from Black clients about resource informations in relation to their accessibility, availability and appropriateness with a view to feeding back their comments to colleagues.

(iv) improving social work 'information system' that can accumulate 'evidence of workable methods,'[58] examples of good policies and planning (e.g. community participation in formulating policies and making decisions about planning resources) and increasing membership of such information system including social work staff and their Black clients.

(v) Use and mobilise professional power to influence policy[59] and procedural resources through 'coalitional' (mutual support and peer reinforcement grouping) power base,[60] that is able to organise 'interest groups' advocating on behalf of clients,[61] that can build 'cooperative relationships' between and among social workers and their cleints instead of 'competing' against each other.[62].

(vi) Engage Black client systems in social work problem-solving[63] by 'recognising' and 'utilising' the strengths of Black families and their communities.

(vii) Engaging Black client systems also refers to making conscious submission of professional specialism to the experience and knowledge base of Black community and voluntary organisations, that have struggled and survived against all odds as valuable resources.

(d) Use institutional structures and mechanisms (e.g. meetings, reports, team work, training, supervision sessions etc.,) as empowering resources for ongoing moral and professional debates on how the principle and practice of social work power are in total contradiction with the principle of caring.

(e) End the 'conspiracy of silence about the presence of racism in social work'[64] and form alliance with voices heard against oppression to build a collective resource that is visible and speaks volumes in favour of social work empowerment.

3. Empowerment as Social Work Practice

(a) Adopt empowerment as an 'explicit goal' and retain a 'firm outcome orientation'[65] of empowering practice; i.e. Client gaining self-power and control.

(b) Start self-examination and self-evaluation of 'internalised feeling of power and powerlessness'[66] and 'ideological self-scrutiny',[67] with a view to developing self-awareness and self-acknowledgement of personal responsibility of either colluding with racist practices or sharing power with clients.

(c) Take initiative and 'risks',[68] be creative and put 'imaginations and experience to work in learning new ways'[69] of changing oppressive practices to empowering practices.

(d) While being innovative, creative, imaginative and taking risks, be confident in 'self-expression' and believe in 'the rightness of these actions'[70] for Black empowerment.

(e) Shift from the traditional views of social work practice and make changes in 'rules of the game',[71] rules that obstruct empowerment of Black clients.

(f) Stop being the 'benefactors' or 'taking on the identity of benefactors' helping 'victims', which by definition perceive the 'benefactors' in a superior status and the 'victims' in an 'inferior' and 'incompetent' position.[72]

(g) Reject those social work skills and techniques that advertently or inadvertently increase the power of social work practice and decrease the self-control and self-dependence of Black clients. Instead develop and apply those empowering social work skills and techniques that promote Black clients' assertiveness in demanding equal services and resources; that heighten their skills to 'manipulate their environment effectively to achieve desired outcomes'; that equip them with 'tactics' of 'threats' and 'disruptions' in 'obtaining needed resources'.[73]

(h) Increase Black clients' power by ensuring that they have information and knowledge of services, resources, entitlements, choices etc., and linking them with those agencies, support network, campaign groups, professionals etc., who are engaged in combatting social inequality and injustice.

(i) Aim for 'normalisation of the exchange differential between expert/ provider and non-expert/supplicant',[74] which –
– does not blame the Black client.
– recognises client's 'previous and ongoing attempted solutions', appreciate his/her reasons of 'failed attempted solutions' to problems and difficulties and perceives their call for social work help as an 'initiative' for 'self-managing in the longer term' instead of defining social work contact as a 'hand over of responsibility' from the Black client to the social worker.

– is aware of the possibility that often for Black clients, 'resistance' or non-cooperation with social work practice is not necessarily a 'defensive' disengagement, but an expression of self-assertion or tactical withdrawal from social work control.
– gives main 'credit for improvements in the problem' to the client.

4. Empowerment as monitoring social work

(a) Assess whether your practice is just a faction of social services 'source of supply', which may not have any relationship with your Black clients, or can the 'nature' of your practice 'involve users', 'safeguard rights', and ensure that your clients' have a 'say in their lives.[75]

(b) Evaluate how your past practices with Black clients and their outcomes reflect your present knowledge base around your principle of empowerment.

(c) Identify what changes you have made in your present practices as a result of (b).

(d) Keep an account of how your 'activities successfully increase the client's power resources rather than the client's conformity to prescribed behaviours', and how your 'intervention technologies focus on mobilizing resources for the client and on environmental changes'.[76]

(e) Accumulate evidences of your actions and practices that make use of your 'professional power' to influence your agencies 'to adopt accountability measures that are based on empowerment principles', not on 'social control'.[77]

(f) Make an inventory of what aspects of your social work practice and intervention are distinctly different from 'existing social work practice', that 'individualises and vacuum-packs social problems' of Black people.[78]

(g) Include those characteristics in your inventory that make you a practitioner, challenging the 'interplay between institutionalised racism and personal suffering' of Black people, advocating for 'organisational changes' and 'initiating changes in individual practices'.[79]

(h) Monitor how your intervention, practice and action have decreased clients' dependency and increased their independence.

(i) Quantify how often your social work practice takes on the campaigning role for racial equality and justice for Black clients (never? sometimes? always?) and qualify how you have done it.

(j) Can your colleagues learn from your campaigning knowledge and experiences? Make a list of what they can learn.

(k) Ensure continuous and simultaneous evaluation of social work practice and social work outcome by Black clients:

– to monitor the credibility and accountability of social work profession in relation to Black communities.
– to identify commonalities and/or differences between professional and client evaluation.
– to reduce gaps of differences between professional and client evaluation without endangering client empowerment.
– to measure client empowerment both from the clients perception of social work outcome and social worker's understanding of client's reality in relation to the outcome.

In introducing this "Checklist For A Radical Social Work Approach," I emphasised its aim directed mainly towards the practitioners. However, the checklist is not just a list of practical guidelines for social work practice with Black clients. Rather, the practical guidelines are based on the ideology of equitable caring and principle of empowerment, that are widely accepted and acknowledged as main objectives of 'Good Social Work Practice' at the present time. Good social work practice must be a concern for all – politicians, managers and practitioners. This checklist then can seek support and endorsement from all, in addition to social work practitioners. This checklist, with its overlapping, interconnecting and reinforcing elements, has the potential for making necessary links between the decision makers and decision carriers, for working towards a collective force that is committed to fulfilling its caring duties and obligations to Black communities.

Turning the Key of Empowerment in Social Work Approach

Some Examples of Good Practice

The history of social work theory and practice has been punctuated by many approaches and will continue to do so in years to follow. In the preceding chapters, I have made reference to Community Social Work approach and different aspects of Empowerment approach. This section illustrates a few examples of good practicé that are identifiable with three other approaches, commonly known as – Task-Centred approach, Unitary approach and Group Work approach.

Empowerment in Task-Centred Approach

In 1969 Reid and Shyne[80] concluded from a research project that short term social casework and intervention could deliver good results in some conditions, if objectives were specified and tasks were planned. During the 70s, Reid, Epstein[81] and their associates developed Task-Centred (T.C.) model of social work that aimed to improve 'direct' social services by taking such measures and following such procedures that could reduce client problems and alleviate target problems perceived by clients. Some of the main principles of effective T.C. social work model are –

1. T.C. should promote efficiency and effectiveness in service delivery.

2. Its outcomes can be measured in relation to achieving improvement.

3. T.C. should ease 'larger probems' even if it can not provide a solution for 'all public welfare problems'.

4. It should operate within 'concrete and explicit goals' directed towards 'target problem/s' based on 'goal-oriented strategy'.

5. 'Goal-oriented strategy' for resolving 'target problem/s' should imply that the 'intervention' and/or 'assisting' procedures and measures are directly related to the problem/s as perceived and experienced by the clients.

6. Procedures and measures of intervention and assistance should then be a two way process, which has scope for shared and complimentary tasks between the client and the practitioner, and above all, which takes account of 'client goal', as opposed to 'professional goal', in particular, those professional goals that are in conflict with client goals.

7. Establishment of close congruence between client and practitioner goal is dependant on assessment of the problems and all problems have a social context[82]; for example environmental conditions, socio-economic status, oppression, experience of discrimination etc. Pre-requisite of T.C. social work assessment then is being adequately aware and informed about all aspects of each of the social context areas and –

(a) identifying which aspects are the root causes of the client problem.

(b) recognising those aspects that precipitate and remain as a continuing source of problem for clients.

(c) acknowledging accumulative effects of aspects that have a long historical context, alongside the social context.

8. T.C. social work should not only be well informed, but also should be able to use its informed assessment and intervention in a way that can explore task alternatives, options and choices and assist the client in deciding what problem to work on and how.

The above principles of T.C. have much potential for empowering clients. Let me demonstrate this by an example of good practice of a school social worker as in *case study* number *8*. For the purpose of this case study I will refer to the social worker as SSW.

Case study 8 – SSW was approached by a school authority to intervene in S family, whose two siblings (ages 9 and 11) had poor and irregular attendance record. At the time of intervention, records showed that the S siblings had not been at school for nearly one whole term. Although, according to the teaching staff home visits were made to find out reasons for non-attendance, no detailed records were kept about the findings of home visits apart from a brief note on "they (children) do not want to come to school . . . parents do not understand they are breaking law . . . they say they will send them (children) to school . . . they come for a few days . . . and back to square one . . . " etc., etc.

The SSW's approach in resolving the problem of non-attendance of S siblings was within the framework of T.C. social work. The account that follows, is presented in the format of questions and answers with references to each of the aforementioned 8 principles, although not in the same order.

Question 1 What were the main considerations for adopting the T.C. approach in resolving the problem of non-attendance?

Answers
(a) Time was an important factor which called for prompt outcome, i.e. improvement in attendance.

(b) There was a strong possibility that the client goal (attending school for educational achievement) and practitioner goal (S siblings attending school) would not be in conflict with each other and as such could set an explicit goal that would be jointly owned.

(c) Most importantly, the SSW concerned had the requisite understanding and knowledge of the environmental and social context of the problem of the S family – the main aspect of which was the notorious occurances of 'Racial Harassment' in the area. This understanding and knowledge equipped the SSW to over-rule any possible subjective assessment of the S family (e.g. ignorant, deviant, irresponsible etc.,) and assess the problem based on the client's perception.

Answers to Q.1 are related to the principles numbers 2, 6 and 7.

Question 2 What was the client's (S family) perception of the problem and how was the T.C. assessment based on the client's perception?

Answers
(a) The client's perception of the problem was based on repeated experiences of both physical and emotional harassments and abuses from a group of white school kids, resulting into the 11 year old being badly beaten up and the 9 year old being terrorised on their way to school and after school.

(b) In order to protect the children, the S family from time to time, arranged to escort the children to and from school, which was not always possible due to personal circumstances.

(c) On two occasions, when the children were escorted to and from school by family friends, some of the white kids followed them home with intimidating gestures. Bricks and wooden planks were thrown through the front room window on the same nights. The S family did not perceive this as coincidental.

(d) The S family made complaints both to the school and the police about these incidents, but did not receive any positive responses. The school's response was that they were not responsible for incidents outside school and the police wanted more concrete evidence!

(e) Combination of all these factors increased the fear and stress of the S family to such an extent that the only option they felt they had in coping with the situation was not to send their young ones to school, however much they wished.

(f) The option chosen did not really ease the stress. Apart from being constantly reminded by the school about the legal consequences of not letting the children attend the school, the S family was concerned about their children not receiving education.

(g) The SSW was the first professional in the experience of the S family that understood their real predicament, which in turn, enabled the SSW to assess the problem on client's perception.

(h) Because the assessment related to the problem as perceived and experienced by the client, it was possible to establish goal-oriented strategy with specific tasks for all concerned, including the S family.

(i) As both the SSW and the S family were fully aware of the enormity and complexities of racial harassment as one of the social evils in Britain, which they alone could not tackle, they adopted a pragmatic approach to achieve a specific goal – children attending school without being exposed to racial harassment and abuse.

Answers to question 2 relate to T.C. principles numbered as 3, 4, 5, 6 and 7 (b) and (c).

Question 3 How were the tasks formulated and shared between the S family and the SSW and how did they compliment each other?

Answers

(a) All the tasks, whether for the family or for the SSW, were formulated around a specific target – return of the children to school as soon as possible.

(b) The SSW's informed assessment and intervention was a key factor in exploring possible and workable task options and variations with the S family.

(c) The exploration made it clear who was best to choose which task options and alternatives and decide on actions relevant to that particular choice and option.

(d) The S family decided to work on their personal difficulties of making regular arrangements of escorting children to and from school – for e.g. taking turns between the parents, making reciprocal arrangements of escorting children with neighbours and/or friends, finding out possibilities of joint transport arrangement with other parents in similar situation depending on the costs, keeping the SSW and the school informed about those days when no arrangements can be made due to unforeseen difficulties and seek temporary help from them on those days and so on.

(e) The SSW in return agreed to find out what supportive measures can be offered to the S family while they were working on their personal difficulties – For e.g. Putting the S family in touch with a local community organisation reputed for its work against racial harassment and known for arranging volunteers to protect community members from racial violence.

(f) Most importantly, the SSW undertook the task of working on a *Professional Contract* with the school (e.g. the Headteacher, Class-teacher), defined in terms of specific conditions to be changed in the school's response to racially motivated bullying and responsibility of dealing with it as part of educational programmes.

(g) Within the framework of the T.C. social work, the establishment of a professional contract was not so much about detailing the various stages of the contract with long term implications, but a short term intervention for creating an environment that began to acknowledge the fear and stress of many parents and children like the S family, who were the victims of racial violence. In relation to the S family, the contract began to dispell the school's negative perception about them and gave them encouraging signals of cooperation from the school in anticipating and tackling obstacles and barriers of racist bullying. In relation to professional accountability and credibility, the contract provided a rationale for directing the attention of the school staff to the prevailing issue of physical violence and abuse. In practical terms, the contract was a starting point for initiating and developing a school strategy for tackling any forms of violence or abuse, whether racially motivated or not.

(h) All members (S family, SSW, School) agreed to keep records of any threats or violence experienced by the children.

(i) There were other interim measures such as – The SSW accompanying the S family and their children to and from school on certain days, the Headteacher and the classteachers making special arrangements for keeping an eye on the S children on their return to school, two school assemblies on 'bullying' before the return of the S children to school etc.

Answers to question 3 relate to T.C. principles numbered as 1, 2, 4, 6, and 8.

If it is not a common practice to make use of mainstream social work approaches in an imaginative way to empower Black clients, then the T.C. social work is perhaps even further removed from creative application of this approach. Yet, the T.C. social work can often be most effective in prompt and efficient delivery of services to Black clients, inspite of some of the constraints of power and resources, limiting the scope of T.C. practice. The T.C. model can enhance social work empowerment as it " . . . requires the social worker to treat the client as an equal, when the client may have little control over the resources he or she requires, when social service procedures emphasise the role of the social worker in rationing, rather than enabling, and when referers expect the social worker to act as a kind of 'nanny' or policeman, or a cross between the two."[83]

Empowerment in Unitary Approach

The concept of Unitary Approach, otherwise known as System or Integrated Approach, gained some social work popularity in the early seventies. At that time, many academics and practitioners such as Pincus and Minahan,[84] Goldstein,[85] Vickery,[86] looked at the implications the Unitary model had for social work theory and practice in general and for specific areas of social work such as Psychology,[87] Group work[88] and Mentally Disordered [89 and 90]. However, no references were made in relation to the implications this model of social work had for Black communities. Although it may be argued that community social work approach has superseded unitary approach, there still exists a notion that the latter has the capacity to provide a framework for practice and expand the horizon of alternative approaches. If it is so, then it is better late than never, to at least consider the empowering aspects of unitary approach for Black people. It is beyond the scope of this section to detail all the implications – thus this section selects empowering characteristics of unitary approach only:

Empowering characteristics of Unitary Approach in social work

1. "The unitary model seeks to integrate the methods of understanding situations traditionally held by caseworkers, group workers and community workers in order to bring about more effective social work intervention. This demand that problems are considered and approached in a variety of ways, and at different levels, in order that we can respond to needs not on the basis of a particular specialism, but on the basis of a considered assessment of the total context of a situation."[91]

2. Assessment of client's problem within the total context of his or her situation requires shifting " . . . the focus of attention from individual or group pathology to that of social interaction"[92] and "material and social environment."[93]

3. In relation to client's social environment, social work practice needs to concern itself with those constraints of social environment that affects clients' ability to "accomplish their life tasks, alleviate distress and realize their aspirations and values. The purpose of social work is therefore to:

(i) Enhance the problem solving capacity of people.

(ii) Link people with the systems that provide them with resources, services and opportunities.

(iii) Promote the effective and humane operation of these systems.

(iv) Contribute to the development and improvement of social policy."[94]

4. Contributing to the development and improvement of social policy means not just shifting "from an individualistic practice perspective to an interactionalist one", but also linking "private ills of individuals . . . to public issues which they may constitute" and "causes of individual client's ills" to the "social structural dimension".[95]

5. The linking process then has direct impacts on social workers' intervention roles, which need not necessarily concentrate exclusively on the client, but extend their intervention roles in their employing agencies, when the ideological basis and structural framework of these agencies are either the main causes of clients' problems, or are contributory factors to vindication of clients' problems.

6. Intervention, whether at client level and/or agency level, "demands considerable knowledge of the various systems affecting individuals and the families in the community", "collecting information", "contacting various elements of the client, target and action systems" in order to collating "data".[96]

7. Social work information and knowledge can be a source of positive power, if there is a "concerted action" meaning that "the attempt to influence problems should be team-based, where appropriate divisions of labour can occur, and where there is at least a possibility of a bit more 'muscle' being available".[97]

8. Positive use of information and knowledge power and concerted action power, inspite of all possible structural and practical restrictions and limitations, can encourage and equip social workers in "taking up the challenges" of increasing pressures on social work profession, instead of "looking for organisational protection against demands from the community."[98]

9. The outward approach that is inherent in challenging has innumerable possibilities of forging alliances with clients and their communities and working towards the empowerment of clients.

Case study 9

SM was a single parent with a history of growing up in institutional care since early childhood. Her only child was on the 'at risk' register of social services, following SM's self-referral for help in child care. The child was given a place in a Day Nursery run by the department. The relationship between SM and the Day Nursery staff was far from good. Records showed that there were several allegations made by the nursery staff against SM, who according to them was 'extremely aggressive', 'provocative and insulting', 'threatening and abusive' etc., etc. Upon rising pressure from the officer-in-charge of the nursery, the department agreed to investigate the allegations. The task of the investigation was delegated to a Section 11 Under Fives adviser, who was one of the members of the Section 11 team in the social services department. The account that follows is not about how the Section 11 Adviser carried out the investigation. Rather, it aims to demonstrate how the aspects of unitary approach turned the investigation process of 'identifying the guilty person/s and apportioning the blame/s to the guilty' into an intervention strategy for locating the real problems between SM and the staff and taking actions for reducing the problems. Readers are advised to make connections between the aforementioned 9 point empowering characteristics of unitary approach and this case study. For the purpose of this case study, I will refer to the Section 11 Adviser as S11A and the Section 11 team as S11T.

Problem

It was obvious from the verbal and written allegations of the nursery staff that they perceived SM as the *Problem* and expected an intervention that would 'successfully modify her behaviour' towards the staff. However, the S11A, after conducting interviews with SM and nursery staff, both separately and jointly, found that SM's behaviour was a manifestation of distress perpetuated by the negative attitude of staff about her. For example, although SM had no access to files and case conference reports, her verbalisation of staff's negative attitude towards her was very similar to the comments recorded in files. This could only mean that the staff, either directly criticised SM or indirectly gave negative vibes to SM making her feel ill at ease. So, the problem could not have been just SM's behaviour. There were professional problems as well.

Assessment

The S11A considered SM's circumstances leading to conflict with the nursery staff. For example her institutional experience of being in care, unhappy experience at school, leaving school without any qualification or career prospect, financial hardships and broken relationships – all these had debilitating effects on her ability to fulfill her life ambitions and aspirations. When she contacted social services department to help her in taking care of her child and was given a nursery place, she saw it as an opportunity for support in enabling her to fulfill her parental role, not as yet another institution 'putting her down'. Her disappointment was manifold – but the one that mattered most was the 'denial of her capacity to be a proper mother'. This she refuted with utmost vigour and contempt as expressed in her 'unsocial behaviour'.

The S11A considered other factors that were common to many young Black women (and men) living in Britain. SM was one of many Black young people who perceive white institutions as authorities ruling their lives and rebel against institutions and authorities as part of their struggle for liberation. The struggle is also about raising 'Black consciousness', and celebrating 'being Black' with pride. Assertion of such struggle, consciousness and celebration is often misconstrued as 'aggressive' or 'provocative' behaviour by white professionals. Unfortunately, the Day nursery staff were all white with the exception of a Black N.N.E.B. student (who interestingly enough had a positive rapport with SM). SM's 'assertive' behaviour was not picked up as a positive strength by the nursery staff.

The S11A's assessment of the situation also considered a 'pattern' that was identified by the S11T in relation to Black clients in the social services. The pattern highlighted some restrained trends in the interactions between most white professionals and most of their Black clients. For example, most White professionals working with Black clients were trapped in an unhealthy anxiety and paranoia combined with insensitivity, unawareness, negative perception, pathology, resistance to change and defensiveness. And most Black clients were enmeshed in an unfavourable suspicion about white proessionals combined with dissatisfaction, feeling of humiliation and anger. The relationship between SM and the day nursery staff reinforced this general pattern of restrained trends.

Intervention

The S11A's intervention was at different levels and varied. Her intervention with SM ranged from direct counselling to linking her with other supporting systems. Other supporting systems included a Black Women's group setting up a community nursery, a local under fives drop-in-centre that had a brilliant track record of providing a variety of supporting services to single parents and a community social worker based in an area office. Readers may be interested to know that SM became actively involved with the Black women setting up the nursery and transferred her child to this nursery later on. Her positive experiences in the drop-in-centre and with the community social worker had significant effects on her behaviour, which remained critical but less abusive.

The S11A's intervention at the Day Nursery was strategical and in two stages. First stage involved preparing a written report, which minimised personalisation and gave an analytical account of the situation based on information and facts gathered during the so called investigation. In addition, the report made recommendations that had implications for all Day Nurseries in the borough. Second stage was aimed at creating an environment for promoting the recommendations and implementing them. The strategies at this stage included establishing a multi-cultural policy framework for all Day Nurseries and developing anti-racist practice guides within the framework. In practical terms, the strategy detailed an implementation programme of:

(a) setting up a working group with memberships from all Day Nurseries, S11T, Users and Other interested individuals with knowledge and experience from statutory and voluntary agencies, with a view to exchanging ideas and putting forward concrete proposals, (SM agreed to be a member of this group as a User);

(b) planning a series of training activities for Day Nursery staff,

(c) building a resource base with useful materials and information,

(d) submitting reports to management teams and relevant council committees.

Team Approach

For S11A application of unitary approach would not have been effective without the S11T. Although this team had all the difficulties inherent in most section 11 appointments (outside mainstream/marginalised/conflicting expectations/without organisational power), it had built up a collective power base that could be positively and tactically used. The collective power base was built on information and knowledge about the local communities and their socio-economic positions, community organisations and resources, local authority structures and procedures, associations and trade unions and race-related institutions and organisations. The team members came from diverse backgrounds with different but complimentary skills and expertise that were shared. Above all, the members were unequivocally committed to the welfare of Black users of social services. This commitment energised their power to taking up the challenges and working constructively.

Any challenging and change efforts need assuring and encouraging support. The S11T provided this support to the S11A, particularly during the first stage of intervention. The team approach was most active in formulating the recommendations in the report prepared by the S11A and throughout the second stage of intervention. To begin with, all intervention strategies were drawn up as a team with careful considerations of team members strengths and weaknesses, their willingness and ability to share different tasks of stage two, their contacts that could be of use in implementing the strategies, and their influences that could ease anticipated hurdles and obstacles.

Outcome

The unitary approach "implies that the change agent must be able to produce some change which is capable of being observed, or really he might have stayed in the office writing memoranda".[99]

The S11A could have just stayed in the office writing report. It probably would have been an easier option than taking on the role of change agent. But would it have been without costs? Costs such as SM and women like her never having the chance to break out of dependancy, hostility and injustice, or under fives' provisions never having a start to keep up with the ever changing community diversities and needs, or social services departments never having to review their outdated policies and practices.

In advocating for the Unitary Approach in "social work with the mentally disordered", Olsen called for "all social workers to have sufficient knowledge and skills in order to conceptualise and practice in a holistic and integrated way; to be able to take account of all systems which affect the individual or group; to identify unmet material need, poor service delivery, and inadequate resources; to promote the application of the rich variety of techniques available to social work on a teamwork and intra- and inter-organisational basis; and to contribute to the improvement and further development of social policy."[100] The S11A's social work intervention encompassed all these and beyond. The Unitary model was also an empowering model for SM and her child.

Critical Appraisal of Unitary Approach

Application of unitary model of social work, without critical appraisal, has little scope for making social work empowering. Ahmed[101] pointed out that the way the unitary model of social work has been advanced "is fundamentally not a radical force. Linked as it is with a systematic model of social work, it rests essentially on a reformist model of social change in which the demands of the disadvantaged working-class communities are managed by state-paid social activists." However, Ahmed identified the "potential" of unitary method "in widening conventional social work practice", which traditionally seeks "explanation of behaviour" in "psychological models" and prefers "casework form of intervention" as opposed to taking "account of the wider social processes". In appraising unitary method of social work Ahmed made two important conclusions – "first that there is certainly a need for a community action approach; but equally importantly, community action needs to be synchronized with clear-cut agency- and service-centred interventions. The former, without the latter, will not be an adequate response."

Critical appraisal of empowering aspects of unitary model of social work needs to analyse the knowledge and value base of all social work approaches, methods and techniques, whether case work, groupwork, community work or community social work. It is not enough to apply a combination of all these approaches, methods and techniques and name it 'unitary', if it is to be empowering. If the knowledge and value base of all social work approaches, methods and techniques are eurocentric, hence racist, then their combined impacts on unitary approach must be profoundly damaging in relation to Black clients and their communities. If social work intervention and assessment skills, applied to Black clients are irrelevant, inappropriate and ineffective, then amalgamation of all these skills within the framework of unitary model must have soaring consequences for Black clients. It is necessary then to analyse eurocentric components of each social work approach, method and technique, to examine adverse outcomes of social work skills, prior to integrating them within a unitary model. This prerequisite presupposes integration of Black perspective as a pivotal component of all methods and practices and as a bedrock for unitary method of social work. So far, for most white social work practitioners, Unitary Approach has been an approach of partial integration without Black perspective. How can a partially integrated model be a unitary model? More importantly, how can a unitary model be empowering without Black perspective? I firmly believe that without Black perspective, Unitary Model of Social Work can neither claim to be an 'Integrated model of Social Work', nor can it fulfill its empowering potentials – whether for Black clients or White clients.

Empowerment in Group Work Approach

Social work profession is not short of group work examples. Group work skill is usually mandatory in all social work education and training courses. Social workers' performance in 'User's groups', 'Client groups', 'Special groups' and many other groups may not have been a pre-occupation in social work, but it is highly regarded as a desired mode of working with people, who are isolated and may need collective support, who are disoriented and dislocated and may benefit from a group experience, and who are disadvantaged and oppressed and may seek collective strength.

There are various definitions of what constitutes groups and different descriptions of types of groups. Definitions of groups are as varied as terminologies describing groups like peer groups, reference groups, interest groups, cultural groups etc., "The one characteristic that is seemingly common to all definitions is that group refers to more than one person."[102] In this context, a social worker can be in a group work setting when s/he is working with more than one person and may decide to do some group work. It is not so much the setting or the number or the decision that matters most in group work with Black clients. There are other factors that are unique to Black clients and different to White clients. This section draws attention of social workers to some of these unique and different factors. Consideration of these factors may be useful in planning and practicing group work with Black clients.

1. In British society, Black clients, by definition, belong to 'minority groups', characterised by racial inequality and discrimination, lack of organisational and institutional power, restricted life opportunities for education and employment, low socio-economic status, other social evils like poverty, poor housing, ill health etc., and experience of racism. It is perhaps not surprising then that, "more than most of the terms commonly used . . . the term 'minority group' generates considerable emotion and difference of opinion about its meaning".[103]

Often, social workers get caught up in emotional and opinionated debates on who belongs to which group, leading nowhere, or ignores the minority status of their Black clients in everywhere. It is worth making note of the reality that whatever the emotions and differences of opinions are, as part of Black communities, Black clients' meaningful membership of any group is dependant on "a shared feeling of peoplehood and a common sense of past and future" and determined by a "sense of belonging" that "connotes cohesion, solidarity, and a basis of identity".[104]

One of the major problems of 'multi-racial' group work has been that the 'groups' are predominantly White, with one or two Black members. As a result, Black members, instead of gaining support and strength, instead of sharing common feelings and aspirations, have found themselves even more isolated and sometimes in threatening situations. In case study 1, I referred to Mrs. B, who was taken to a women's refuge and experienced much stress. I pointed out how many women like Mrs B. experience pressure for joining groups and stress of unease and unwelcome after joining groups encouraged by social workers; how Black members 'drop out' from groups. So often I hear disappointing remarks from social workers about 'ethnic minority people not being group oriented', 'reluctant to join groups', 'prefer to stay at home', 'keep themselves to themselves'. Yet several directories of Black and minority ethnic groups (many groups are not included in the directories) prove the contrary. These comments demonstrate a lack of understanding of the limitations of group work with Black clients in an environment of white dominance. Moreover, even in those group work settings, where there is a numerical parity between Black and White members, there may be different perceptions about common issues that are difficult or impossible to share; there may be group dynamics that undermine Black members' experience and contributions, there may even be clash of interests and priorities between Black and White members. 'Multi-racial' group work needs to be prepared to deal with these shortcomings and pitfalls. Otherwise, group work, however inadvertantly, will just collude with social work control of Black clients, even though in the disguise of group work.

2. Preparation for dealing with shortcomings and pitfalls of multi-racial group work is the main responsibility of the group worker, particularly at the initial stage. First, the group workers must be clear of why they want their Black clients to join a group and how will their Black clients benefit from a group experience. They must check whether their Black clients share the same objectives or have different perceptions of group work needs and benefits. This means spending considerable time with the clients at an individual level to ensure that group work is not imposed on Black clients, that they are able to decide for themselves whether they want to join a group or not, that they have the confidence of joining a group, and most importantly, they determine the terms and conditions of joining a group. Second, the group workers must have certain ground rules and principles for all multi-racial group work methods – for example non-accpetance of racist behaviour and gestures, non-entry of negative and offensive Black images, non-patronising environment, respect for Black members, format for Black voices to be heard, and separate time and space for Black members whenever necessary. This means working with the White members individually and in groups.

3. In many instances multi-racial group work may not be appropriate for some Black clients. "This is partly due to the problem of communi-

cation and the inability to understand different cultural and social frames of reference. But it is mostly due to the fact that such projects have made most black people feel uneasy, if not unwelcome, since the most well-intentioned attempts at bringing people together were invariably set against the background of sustained hostility towards minority groups that made them cautious of any contact with white society and its institutions."[105] Mixed groups often inhibit Black members' freedom of cultural expressions, misplace their social frame of reference and minimise their Black identity and pride. There is now enough evidence to suggest that many Black clients have gained tremendous support and strength from Black groups. Promotion of black groups for Black clients must be an alternative group work approach.

4. Traditionally, social workers tend to use group work method as an extended social work intervention with a therapeutic bias. Group work values are usually based on a belief that in a group setting clients can vent their 'feelings' amongst others with similar or same problems and get a 'relief'; in exchanging feelings about their problems they can gain some 'comfort' realising that 'they are not the only one who has problems'; and in sharing their problems they can 'give support to each other'. Within this context, the style of group work is 'group therapy' oriented and group work skill has 'group counselling' tenet. Therapeutic group work has its merits in some circumstances. But as far as empowerment is concerned, it offers very little. More often than not, problems of Black clients (and other oppressed groups), are rooted to wider social problems over which they have little or no control. Consequently, they (oppressed groups) concern themselves with wider issues. This concern can be constructively used by group workers as an incentive for 'group action'. Group workers can learn from many examples of the most disadvantaged, ostracised, down-trodden and discriminated clients, forming their own groups and using them as instruments for asserting their rights, campaigning for services, and pushing for change. While advocating for a particular approach of working with small groups, which Mullender and Ward (1989) called 'self-directed groupwork', they quoted examples of group workers from field and residential social work, playing "a part in an exciting user revolution, which has transcended traditional client group boundaries".[106]

5. Black communities have a long history of struggling for equality, fighting for freedom and campaigning for justice. This long history in itself is an evidence of their ability to form groups and forging self-directed group actions. Social workers need not worry about their Black clients' ability to function in a group setting. Rather, they should inform themselves with the knowledge of Black self-help groups that are providing valuable services, including services to Black communities; that a large number of these groups are managed and run by Black people for Black people; that many of these groups are 'user' groups as members are from either ex or existing 'client groups' of social services.

Knowledge of these group work activities in Black communities will not only widen the mainstream group work approaches, but also will enable group workers to use this knowledge to empower their Black clients by giving them options and choices, through resourcing Black group work initiatives and supporting them.

6. Resourcing and supporting Black group work initiatives require specific group work skills. For example,

(a) listening skill that hears the Black voice and does not interpret Black words;

(b) communication skill that has a rapport with Black experience and does not misconstrue Black reality;

(c) facilitating skill that makes maximum use of Black strength and minimises portrayal of weakness;

(d) influencing skill that can raise the profile of Black aspirations and expectations and does not misrepresent them;

(e) leadership and liaising skills that are applied for convincing others who can provide support and resources and are not used for directing Black groups;

(f) advocacy skill that has the confidence of Black group/s and ability to elucidate concern of these groups to agencies for support and resource;

(g) organising skill that can obtain useful contacts, information and resources for these group/s.

(h) servicing skill that can be used by group/s as a resource for practical and maintenance purposes such as venue, refreshments, transport, paper work etc.

Some Examples of Empowering Group Work

Black Children

"I can't face this life alone
'cos I've always lived in a home
Thrown out at seventeen
with no friends or family
Thank-you social services
for your hospitality.
Here I am in a black community
I've grown up 'white' but they can't see.
Which do I turn to – white or black?
I daren't step forward, I can't step back
Help me someone please
To find my culture and identity
Why could I not have these when I was young?

They brought me up to think being black is wrong.
Black people out there
You've got to be aware
For its bad for your child to be in care."

Margaret Parr[107]

Margaret Parr's poem sums up the predicament of hundreds of Black children in care and the justification for setting up the group of Black and In Care (BIC). BIC is composed of young Black people in care and ex-care. Since 1984 BIC has been actively involved in pressurising "local authorities for improved policies and conditions, and for basic changes in the attitudes of 'professionals' who must be prepared to acknowledge their own racism and must also be prepared actually to implement progressive changes."[108] BIC's conference report of 1984 gives a vivid account of its aims and aspirations for self-pride, self-control and self-realisation. Its challenging slogan of 'Black families for black children' has been the main driving force for promoting 'same race placement' policies and recruitment practices of Black foster and adoptive parents.

The Ebony group which was set up for young Black people in White foster homes, used group work approach "to raise level of black self-awareness and pride, and of cultural and racial knowledge, and also to help develop survival skills against racism."[109] Group work methods included learning Black history, knowledge of Black achievements, face to face interaction with Black group leaders, Black role models, etc.

Black Elders

In a North London Borough, a group of Black elders used to meet in a church building once a week for religious gathering and chanting. Gradually, their membership grew in numbers from 6/8 to 20/30, as news about this small group spread through their community network. Soon the purpose for meeting together ceased to be just religious. They began to discuss their needs and articulate their demands for a regular meeting place with day care and leisure facilities. With the help of a Black social worker and community leaders, they succeeded in obtaining resources from local autority departments; for example a premise from the housing department, small capital grant from the community development department, and finance from the social services department for luncheon club. As they proceeded step by step with all their plannings and authority's procedures, they formed their own management committee and established themselves as a viable group. The group members shared various tasks of setting up the day centre and luncheon club, buying equipments and furnitures, and recruiting a cook and volunteers. The luncheon club became quite a popular meeting and eating place not just for elders, but for community members and council employees. Only difference was that others paid more for food than the elders.

This is only one of many other examples, where Black elders, given the opportunity, support and resources, have organised themselves in self-help groups. Most of these groups are in Black community organisations like churches, temples, gurdwaras and community centres. The problems these groups face are not lack of community interest or group work skills. Their main problems are mainstream agencies, both statutory and voluntary, who have a record of abdicating from their responsibility to support and resource these groups. Without support and resource, these groups remain most vulnerable and their empowering prospects are severely hindered.

Black Women

Like Black elders, Black women have extensively used group work methods to deal with their family and social problems. Lunn's report[110] of Project Pehchan is a reflection of nearly all Black women's groups, who do not see themselves as 'problem-oriented' groups, but more as 'creative' and 'preventative' groups. In an advise and resource centre in Birmingham, women workers' group work approach in working with a group of 'battered' women had empowering effects on some of these women, who began to take active part in managing their 'refuge', giving advice to other women, running industrial language classes and organising trips and other leisure activities. Leicester's Black women counselling group is yet another example of Black women organising their own 'counselling' group, where some counsellors are users of services as well. So is a Black women's group in Manchester dealing with family violence and child abuse. Fundamental principle that is common to most Black women self-help groups is that they have their empowering agenda within the framework of their historical and cultural experiences. White social workers, particularly white feminist social workers, often perceive this historical and cultural framework as being oppressive and discourage their Black women clients from joining these groups. Nothing could be more disempowering than such discouragements of Black women joining Black women's groups. Because it is the most vulnerable and most trodden Black women that can gain much from a group experience that is more in tune with their background and culture. This must be of paramount consideration for all group workers.

Health

One of the main casualties of racism and discrimination is poor health. There is now considerable evidence of Black communities adversely effected by mortality, prenatal and infant mortality, obstetric health inequality, mental ill health and ill health specific to Black people.[111] For a long time Black communities have pressed for improving their health conditions and adequate services. Their campaign for good health has not just been directed towards health institutions. They have taken their health issues right to the heart of their communities. In so doing, they have formed groups to raise awareness of their community members about health related matters and develop community health programmes. Nearly all these group function with virtually no resources or temporary facilities. Had there not been relentless commitment from group members, there would be no Black health groups left in Britain today. What a loss it would have been if that was the case. Quoting a few examples of Black health groups do not do justice to the enormous contributions made by these groups. The examples are quoted in this section more as an acknowledgement than an account.

Example 1 In response to a growing concern of a group of Cypriot women, two social workers in their area made necessary arrangements for the group to meet in the area office once a week and serviced the group in developing its interest and maintenance. The group became a central focus for discussing health issues affecting these women and their families, in particular thalassaemia. Its impact on the Cypriot community, struggling to find resources for dealing with thalassaemia, was significant. It may seem over rated to conclude that successful application for section 11 funding for a Thalassaemia Worker in the community was entirely due to this group's activity. But it will be equally under rated to dismiss the contribution of this group to its community. The group was an active partner of community action that expedited response from social services and health authority.

Example 2 Organisation for Sickle Cell Anaemia (OSCAR) is a glowing example of community group action. Despite the prevalence of sickle cell anaemia amongst Afro-Caribbean communities, health and other welfare institutions failed to address this crucial health issue for a long time. If it was not for Black groups organising themselves for concerted action and pressure, there would not be any research or information available on sickle cell anaemia.[112]

Example 3 Black groups for mental ill health is on the rise. Once gain, the formation of these groups is a clear declaration of taking control of those health issues that have devastating consequences for Black communities. Empowerment of Black mental health is the key focus of these groups as expressed so eloquently by Gabriel[113] in relation to an 'empowerment group' of 'chronically mentally disordered people' and a 'psychotherapy group' of 'survivors'. Central aims of this group work method are – "to provide an atmosphere of support in which race and culture are validated and positively regarded", to facilitate "empowerment of clients to articulate their needs and generate their own resources", and to disprove "the white middle class theory that black people and schizophrenics have insufficient cognitive and behavioural skills to make use of psychotherapy."

Disabled

"As far as disability is concerned, people tend not to want to know about race or racism. In considering provision they do not think they will need to think any more specifically than in terms of disability alone." (quotation from an Interviewee from a Report of Confederation of Indian Organisation U.K. entitled "*Double Bind to be disabled and Asian*")

Perhaps the most neglected area that is drawing growing attention of caring professionals is Black people with disability. There is a dearth of information about the extent of disability in Black communities and little knowledge of the nature of services available to Black disabled. From time to time disturbing incidents come to light causing concern. Many Black famlies with disabled family members do not even get to know about benefits and allowances, let alone receiving aids and grants. Even when some disabled Black people get access to services their cultural and social needs are not met.

Case study 10 – The family of severely handicapped Young Z was delighted when respite care for their daughter was arranged. After some time Young Z seemed very withdrawn (she was usually very lively) on return from respite care and became very upset when her next visit was due. Respite carers assured her parents that there were no problems with Young Z and that she would settle down to the routine eventually. She didn't. So her parents decided to collect her earlier than the agreed time. They found Young Z sitting in her night clothes in the middle of the day looking more withdrawn than ever. Her parents queried what was wrong with their daughter. Carers responded spontaneously 'Oh nothing – she does mind wearing her nightie all day – you see your clothes are so difficult to put on – they are ethnic aren't they – she is much more comfortable in her nightie'! Young Z loved wearing her so called 'ethnic clothes'. Besdies she was the only one who had to spend all her respite stay in her bed clothes. Imagine her feeling of indignity and humiliation.

Case study 11 – In an elderly people's home only one resident was a Black elderly man. The staff group was totally White, whose "misconception" about the man's expression of religious beliefs and "literal interpretation of his spoken words" exacerbated the tension between the staff and the Black elder. In a case conference, this tension was verbalised by the staff through comments like 'he is violent . . . he is like a mechanical dog'. The label of 'violent' was due to the fact that the man, in refusing to eat bacon for religious faith, threw his plate from the table. The label of 'mechanical dog' was referred to the man 'walking into furnitures and walls'. The fact was that following the 'bacon' incident, the staff took away his stick. He was "totally visually handicapped"![11]

Although not in many numbers, Black and minority ethnic groups for disabled people are emerging steadily. One such group is Association of Blind Asians. The group is managed entirely by the blind and partially sighted people. The motivation that formed the group was based on a knowledge that Minority blind people were not receiving services from their local authorities. Within three years the group's membership increased to 250. This in itself indicates the need for Association of Blind Asians.

Reference

1. L. Sissay (1985) – *Black Rap – Black and In Care Conference Report – Children's Legal Centre* – Blackrose Press (TU) 1985.

2. F. A. Zewig – *Welfare Workers – Through Different Eyes, Eds.* Rose, Rothman and Wilson.

3. *The Soul Kids Campaign* – Waterloo Press Ltd., 1977.

4. Commission for Racial Equality – *A Home from Home? Some policy considerations for black children in residential care 1977.*

5. *Home Affairs Select Committee Report on Racial Disadvantages* – HC 424 – HMSO 1981.

6. H. Ousley – *The System* – Runnymede Trust 1981.

7. I. D. Batta and R. I. Mawby – *Children in Local Authority Care: A Monitoring of Racial Difference in Bradford, Policy and Practice, vol. 9, no. 2, 1981.*

8. ABSWAAP – *Black Children in Care* – Evidence to the House of Commons Social Services Committee 1983.

9. ibid no. 1.

10. Commission for Racial Equality – *Probation and After-Care In A Multi-Racial Society 1981.*

11. National Association for the Care and resettlement of Offenders – *Black People And the Criminal Justice System 1986.*

12. Home Office – *Ethnic Minorities in Borstal 1981.*

13. L. K. Hemsi – *Psychiatric mobility of West Indian immigrants* – Social Psychiatry 2, 1967.

14. F. Hashmi – *Community Psychiatric Problems Among Birmingham Immigrants* – International Journal of Social Psychiatry 2, 1968.

15. R. T. Pinto – *A Study of Psychiatric Illness Among Asians in the Camberwell Area* – Unpublished M.Phil *Dissertation in Psychiatry* – University of London 1970.

16. C. Bagley – *Mental illness in immigrant minorities in London* – Journal of Bisocial Science 3, 1971.

17. J. Giggs – *High Rates of Schizophrenia Among Immigrants in Nottingham* – Nursing Times (20.9.1973).

18. R. Cochrane – *Mental illness in immigrants to England and Wales*: An analysis of mental hospital admissions – Social Psychiatry 12, 1977.

19. L. Carpenter & I. F. Brockington – *A study of mental illness in Asians, West Indians and Africans living in Manchester* – British Journal of Psychiatry 137, 1980.

20. P. Hitch – *The Policies of Intervention in Asian Families* – 1980 Bulletin of Transcultural Psychiatry Society (UK), March 1981.

21. A. Shaikh – *Cross-cultural comparison; psychiatric admission of Asian and Indigenous patients in Leicestershire* – International Journal of Social Psychiatry 31, 1985.

22. D. McGovern & R. Cope – *First psychiatric admission rates of first and second generation Afro-Caribbeans* – Social Psychiatry 122, 1987.
23. A. W. Burke – *Racism. Prejudice and Mental Illness – Transcultural Psychiatry* Ed. J. Cox – Croom Helm 1986.
24. S. Fernando – *Race And Culture In Psychiatry* – Croom Helm 1988.
25. M. Abrams – *Profiles of the Elderly* – Age Concern 1977.
26. M. Anwar – *The Myths of Return: Pakistanis in Britain* – Heinemann 1979.
27. A. Bhalla & K. Blakemore – *Elders of the ethnic minority groups – Affor (All Faiths for One Race)* study – Birmingham 1981.
28. F. Glendenning – (ed.) – *The Elders in Ethnic Minorities* – Beth Johnson Foundation Publication, 1979 and *Ethnic Minority Elderly People: Some Issues of Social Policy* – Social work and Ethnicity – Ed. J. Cheetham – Allen & Unwin 1982.
29. J. Barker – *Black and Asian Old People in Britain* – Age Concern 1984.
30. *The Standing Conference of Ethnic Minority Senior Citizens* – First Report 1984 and Second Report 1989.
31. A. Norman – *Triple Jeopardy: growing old in a second homeland* – Centre for Policy on Ageing – 1985.
32. S. Chiu – *Chinese Elderly People: No Longer A Treasure At Home* – Social Work Today – 10.8.1989.
33. P. Ely & D. Denney – *Social Work in a Multi-Racial Society* – Gower 1987.
34. P. Roys – *Social Services – Britain's Black Population A New Perspective*, Ed. Bhat, Carr-Hill & Ohri – Gower 1988.
35. B. B. Solomon – *Black Empowerment: social work in oppressed communitoes* – Columbia 1976.
36. Y. Hasenfeld – *Power in Social Work Practice* – Social Service Review – University of Chicago, September 1987.
37. S. Croft & P. Beresford – *Time For Social work to Gain New Confidence* – Social Work Today, April 1989.
38. G. Mitchell – *Empowerment and Opportunity* – Social Work Today, March 1989.
39. ibid no. 38.
40. J. L. Russell-Erlich & F. G. Rivera – *Community Empowerment as a Non-Problem* – Community Development Journal vol. 22, no. 1, 1987.
41. ibid no. 37.
42. J. H. Cones – *Black Theology and Black Power* – New York – Seabury Press, 1969
43. ibid no. 40.
44. ibid no. 36.
45. ibid no. 35.
46. L. Dominelli – *Anti-Racist Social Work* – BASW – Macmillan 1986.
47. ibid no. 36.
48. ibid nos. 36 & 37.
49. ibid no. 37
50. ibid no. 36.

51. ibid no. 46.
52. ibid no. 35.
53. M. Furlong – *A Rationale for the use of Empowerment as a Goal in Casework* – Australian Social work – vol. 40, no. 3, September 1987.
54. ibid no. 36.
55. ibid no. 36.
56. ibid no. 40.
57. ibid no. 46.
58. ibid no. 40.
59. ibid no. 46.
60. W. R. Sherman and S. Wenocur – *Empowering Public Welfare Workers through Mutual Support* – Social Work 28 – September/October 1983.
61. ibid no. 36.
62. ibid no. 40.
63. ibid no. 35.
64. ibid no. 46.
65. ibid no. 53.
66. R. L. Hegar and J. M. Hunzeker – *Moving toward Empowerment-Based Practice in Public Child Welfare* – Social Work 33 (6) – November/December 1988.
67. ibid no. 38.
68. ibid no. 66.
69. ibid no. 40.
70. ibid no. 66.
71. ibid no. 40.
72. ibid no. 66.
73. ibid no. 36.
74. ibid no. 53.
75. ibid no. 37.
76. ibid no. 36.
77. ibid nos. 36 and 46.
78. ibid no. 46.
79. ibid no. 46.
80. W. J. Reid and A. W. Shyne – *Brief and extended casework* – Columbia University Press, 1969.
81. W. J. Reid and L. Epstein – *Task-centred practice* – Columbia University Press, 1977.
82. A. Vickery – *How to Provide social Services With Task-Centred Methods* (A British Adaptation) – NISW Papers no. 13, 1981.
83. E. M. Goldberg, J. Gibbons and I. Sinclair – *Problems, Tasks and Outcomes – The evaluation of task-centred casework in three settings – NISW Social Services Library no. 47* – Allen & Unwin, 1985.
84. A. Pincus and A. Minahan – *Social Work Practice: Model and Method* – F. E. Peacock, Itasca, Illinois, 1973.
85. H. Goldstein – *Social Work Practice: A Unitary Approach*, University of South Carolina Press, 1973.
86. A. Vickery – *Use of Unitary Models in Education for Social*

Work – Integrating Social Work Methods – Eds. Specht and Vickery – Allen and Unwin, 1977.
87. J. Ellis – *Psychology and the Unitary Approach to Social Work: Some issues for the Curriculum – The Unitary Model* – BASW Publications 1978.
88. L. Muir – *An Application of the Unitary Approach in Group Work* – ibid no. 87.
89. A. Vickery – *A Unitary Approach to Social Work with the Mentally Disordered – Differential approaches in Social Work with Mentally Disordered* – ed. M. R. Olsen – BASW publications 1976.
90. M. R. Olsen – *Social Work with Mentally Disordered – The Need for a Unitary Practice* – ibid no. 87.
91. R. Currie and B. Parrott – *A Unitary Approach to Social Work – Application in Practice* – BASW publications 1981.
92. R. Wilkes – *Some Philosophical implications of the Unitary Approach* – ibid no. 87.
93. R. J. Evans – *Unitary Models of Practice and the Social work Team* – ibid no. 87.
94. ibid no. 84.
95. ibid no. 93.
96. ibid nos. 91 and 93.
97. B. Sheldon – *Social Influence: Social Work's Missing Link* – ibid no. 87.
98. ibid no. 91.
99. P. Baird – *The Evaluation of Social work Practice* – ibid no. 87.
100. ibid no. 90.
101. S. Ahmed – *Setting up a community Foster Action Group – Race and Social Work* – Eds. Coombe and Little – Tavistock Publications, 1986.
102. ibid no. 35.
103. W. Devore and E. G. Schlesinger – *Ethnic-Sensitive Social Work Practice* – Merrill Publishing Company (2nd edition) 1987.
104. ibid no. 103.
105. R. Sondhi – *The Asian Resource Centre – Birmingham – Community Work and Racism* – Eds. Ohri, Manning and Curno – Routledge and Kegan Paul, 1982.
106. A. Mullender and D. Ward – *Gaining Strength Together* – Social Work Today 24.8.1989.
107. M. Parr – *Its bad for your child to be in care* – ibid no. 1.
108. K. Williams – *Foreword* ibid no. 1.
109. A. Mullender – *Groupwork As the Method of Choice With Black children in White Foster Homes* – Groupwork vol. 1. no. 2 eds. Brown & Kerslake, 1988.
110. T. Lunn – *Leaving The Lump* – Community Care – 17.8.1989.
111. M. Grimsley and A. Bhat – *Health* – ibid no. 34.
112. P. Clarke and N. Clare – *Sickle-Cell Anaemia: A Challenge to Health Education* – Health Education Council Journal, vol. 40, no. 2, 1981.
113. S. Gabriel – *Black To Black* – Community care, Race and Mental Health 3, 12.10.1989.

114. A. Ahmad – *Social services for Black People – service or lip service* – Published by Race Equality Unit – personal social services (National Institute for Social Work) August 1988.

Chapter 3
Resources for Change

In most professions the word 'change' surfaces considerable emotions – negative and positive. For some, 'change' means excitement, adventure, new initiative, refreshing direction, revitalised energy and most importantly new hope for future. For some others, 'change' gives rise to feeling unsure and insecure, instils fear of giving up years of habit at the risk of being exposed to incompetence, or losing familiarity at the expense of lost comfort. In relation to change for race equality, for many, 'change' is too challenging or too threatening. Yet working towards race-equality is about making shift from unequal boundaries to equal premises, which is not possible without making 'change' a continuing theme in all aspects of professional policies and practices.

I have mentioned before about the incompatibility of the caring profession and racial inequality. I have stressed on how social work has no option but to eradicate the non-caring effects of racism from its professional ethos and practice. In the previous chapters I have commented on social work theories and practices and have given examples of how social work profession can achieve change for equality. This section builds on the previous sections and develops them further with specific reference to resources – resources that can be generated or controlled by social workers in transforming their 'non-caring' practice to 'caring practice'.

Good Practice as a Resource for Change

The most valuable resource for social work change for racial equality is 'good practice'. Generally, resource is perceived as quantifiable objects, that one can see, touch, hold, gain or lose. In institutional terms, resources are something that can either be allocated, reallocated, misallocated or increased and decreased. Resource of good practice, although not totally detached from quantifiable resources, can be, to a great extent, independent of the constraints of quantifiable resources. The cardinal factor that can make resource of good practice independent is practitioner's performance. Social work performance of good practice is dependent on each professional's commitment and ability to fully seek and utilise all the necessary components of anti-racist practice resources. The necessary components of good practice resource are:

1. Developing awareness, understanding and knowledge of issues that have direct or indirect implications for Black clients or consumers.

2. Gaining experience of transferring awareness, understanding and knowledge to social work method and approach, and intervention and prevention.

3. Acquiring skills of identifying real needs (what to look for and from where), assessing (how to do it and what actions are going to empower the Black client), and evaluating (what are the empowering aims and how are they achieved).

4. Establishing a code (in the absence of organisational code establish your own personal code) for professional responsibility and accountability that can appraise professional learning and development; monitor and measure social work outcome.

5. Exchanging information and expertise and expanding support network to maintain progress and promote it and to avoid the cost of 'reinventing the wheel'.

6. Planning ahead for minimising reactive social work and keeping abreast with pro-active social work.

It must be apparent from the five points above that non-racist practice is good social work practice and good social work practice is good for all, whether Black or White.

Planning for Practice as a Resource for Change

Planning for practice as an anti-racist resource for change is a simultaneous process of an action plan that has two major targets. One of the two targets is permeation of non-racist practice in all aspects of planning. The other target is specific planning, in addition to overall planning, that can redress the accumulated deficit and past imbalance. This means planning for 'positive' or 'affirmative' practice.

Affirmative practice is not about discriminating in favour of Black clients and disfavouring White clients and 'reversing discrimination'. On the contrary, it is about condoning and ensuring equity in social work planning for practice. It is about acknowledging the fact that as a result of past experiences of oppression and discrimination, Black clients have an accumulation of deficit. It is about redressing this deficit with affirmative practice, without which the gap of inequality will continue to widen, leaving Black clients even further behind. A working definition of Affirmative practice (action) is – 'the development of programmes which provide in detail for specific steps to guarantee equal opportunities going beyond passive notions of non-discrimination and including where there are major deficiencies, the development of specific goals and timetables for the prompt achievement of full and equal opportunities.' The following diagram is based on this definition and is related to the dual planning of permeating and redressing models of social work practice.

Diagramme 2

Affirmative Practice

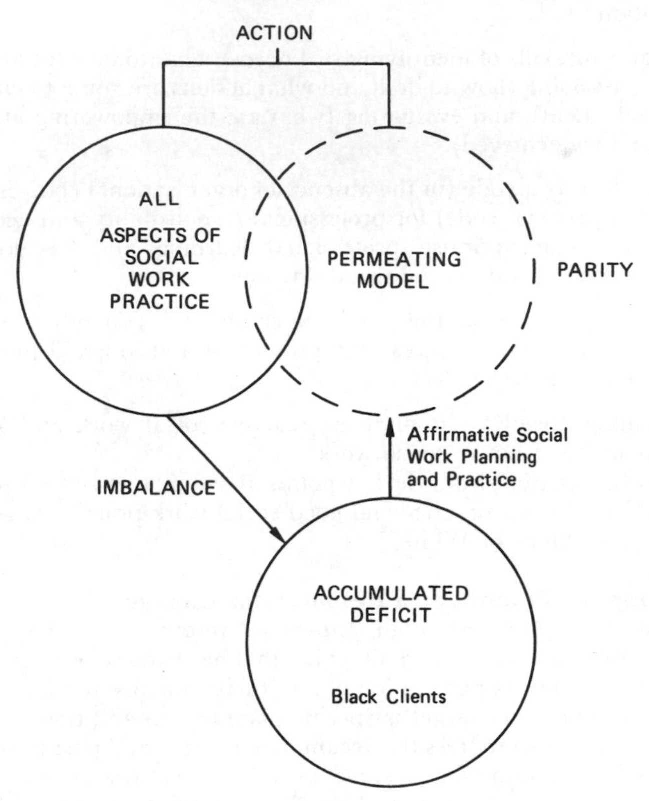

A personal planning of Affirmative practice may mean:

1. Making personal time for working on the five components of good practice resource, mentioned in the preceding section.

2. Identifying 'major deficiencies' in personal practice and acting on them.

3. Having specific personal goal and a timetable to achieve the goal (it can be as specific as reading a book on for example on Black history).

4. Analysing the differences between Black and White clients with same or similar problems.

5. Taking an aggressive step from a 'colour bind' (e.g. if the problem is the same or similar then its impact on both Black and White clients is the same) approach to an 'ethnically sensitive' (e.g. impact is both common and different) approach.

6. Changing personal values and pre-conceived notions and making a personal note of these changes (e.g. inarticulation of changes may neither 'guarantee going beyond passive notion of non-discrimination', nor evaluate quality of practice).

Extend this list and move them upwards to the permeating model. Remember that it is a continuous process, not just an occasional activity or a one-off exercise. The process of change in itself is a resource for change.

Black Community as a Resource for Change

In 1968, para 474 of the Seebohm committee Report (followed by the Social Services Act 1970) commented – "At many points in this report we have stressed that we see our proposals not simply in terms of organisation but as embodying a wider conception of social service, directed to the well-being of the whole of the community and not only of social casualities, and seeing the community it serves as the basis of its authority, resources and effectiveness." In 1970, welcoming the seventh meeting of the British National Conference on Social Welfare, the Rt Hon. George Thomas made reference to the then Green Paper on The Future Structure of the National Health service and the White Paper on Reform of Local Government in England and stated, "The challenge for the future of our social services in the 1970s is an enormous one. The attainment of a fully participating society is a goal which we cannot afford to fail to achieve."[2] In 1986, The Runnymede Trust study pointed out that – "Insensitivity to the needs and aspirations of minorities has resulted in their relative absence from consultation and participation in mainstream programmes. In many areas black and other ethnic minority groups claim that their needs have never been considered by local authorities, and have strongly argued for direct consultation and involvement in the decision-making process."[3]

A snap shot of these 18 years suggests that consultation with and participation of Black communities in social services have not yet fully adhered to Seebohm's and Thomas's pledge for community participation and perceiving community as a resource. But then again, very few mainstream reports and papers (legislations as well) relate to Black and minority ethnic communities. As if reference to 'communities' just imply White communities as a rule. However, in the recent years, consideration of Black communities as part of the whole community has received due attention in some quarters. For example, CRE[4] found that 34 social services departments had consulted 'ethnic minority groups in reaching a decision about priority service areas'. Specific mentions of 'ethnic minority communities' are also made in the White paper on Community Care[5] and Children Act 1989.[6] This is both encouraging and welcoming. Social workers must grab this as an opportunity to steer ahead and make maximum use of Black communities as a resource for change. I have given accounts of the strengths of Black communities in Britain in each and every section. I have quoted many examples of their knowledge, their experience and their expertise that can enhance social work practice in each chapter. I have suggested some possible ways which Social workers can adopt in empowering their Black clients. All these accounts, examples and suggestions are linked to Black community participation and consultation. Departmental structures of community participation and consultation are essential and useful; but they are not the be all and end all. Besides, like most departmental structures, consultative mechanisms usually take place either in the higher management and commitee level or at the periphery of social services. Either way, the possibility is that social workers in general, may not be a part of these structures and mechanisms. It is all the more reason then that every social worker build their own participatory and consultative network with their Black communities not for exploiting the contributions made by black communities, or for abdicating from personal responsibilities, but for making positive use of this network as a resource for change.

Black Voluntary Organisations as a Resource for Change

"The black community was so much better organized and equipped than the white community in Philadelphia for caregiving that the white community turned to the black community for salvation when Philadelphia was plagued by an epidemic of yellow fever in 1793."[7]

The role of voluntary organisations providing valuable welfare services has been greatly appreciated by politicians, managers, practitioners and most importantly by users for many years. This appreciation is well justified, as indeed, the long history and experience of Britain's voluntary organisations have been significant in influencing and shaping much of todays social policies and social services institutions. In so doing, as Britain's voluntary organisations have provided direct services to those in need, they have been indispensible as well, in complimenting and subsidising statutory services, in bridging the gaps that have not been addressed or tackled by statutory agencies. Often, they have been the backcloth of social concern, where users, professionals and policy makers from all sectors have been able to bring social issues to light; express concerns, in particular those concerns that are not well received in a statutory climate; and campaign for social change. Overall, the relationship between British statutory and voluntary organisations has been exciting and productive.

The relationships between British organisations, both statutory and voluntary, and Black voluntary organisations are however different. There are apparent and evidential similarities between the relationships of Black organisations and statutory bodies and Black organisations and mainstream (white) voluntary organisations. The similarities are most explicit in for example, like statutory institutions, mainstream voluntary organisations are predominantly White, both in relation to white people's dominance in management structures and workforce and white prevalence in users of services. The way the services are designed (ethos) and provided (practical arrangements) by most mainstream voluntary organisations, makes these service provisions unattractive, unaccessible and inappropriate for Black users, leading to poor or non-existent take up of services from Black consumers. The similarities are also explicit in 'Black and White' power relationship, which juxtaposes statutory institutions and mainstream voluntary organisations much closer, compared to the status and position of Black voluntary organisations. In this context, the status and position of Black voluntary organisations are much closer to Black client groups in need of services than their White counterparts. In other words, Black organisations are also victims of racism and racial discrimination. As a result, as opposed to most mainstream voluntary organisations, nearly all Black organisations do not have security of core funding or stable resources, do not receive consistent statutory support and do not get the opportunities for forming real partnerships with white organisations. It is inevitable then that most White initiated and white dominated voluntary organisations have a "headstart" working against the interest of Black voluntary organisations.[8]

Against all these odds, Black voluntary organisations have struggled to survive and have voiced their dissatisfaction in services provided (or not) by white agencies. But most importantly, they have been engaged in establishing alternative services for their communities.

In September 1988, the Race Equality Unit based at the National Institute for Social Work, organised a major conference for Black voluntary organisations providing welfare services. More than 70 organisations from different parts of England and Wales attended the conference. The main aims were:

– to listen to their experience,
– to identify their roles,
– to take account of their expectations and aspirations,
– to formulate proposals for future actions, and
– to acknowledge their contributions.

The aims were based on seven fundamental assumptions. They were:

"– The emergence of black voluntary organisations is a direct outcome of a lack of appropriate and adequate mainstream service provision for black communities.

– Black organisations provide alternative services to black communities as well as subsidising and/or complementing statutory services.

– Most black organisations deal with all aspects of community needs rather than dealing only with a specific need, for example disability.

– Even those black organisations dealing with a particular need such as mental health, operate within the framework of a comprehensive approach (responding to all other needs, such as housing, employment, education and so on) instead of compartmentalising and categorising 'special' needs.

– Most black organisations have little or no regional boundaries.

– Black organisations have severely restricted resources and insecurity compared to most mainstream voluntary organisations.

– Compared to other mainstream agencies the management and employees of black voluntary organisations lack opportunities for training, appropriate terms and conditions of employment and as such are most vulnerable."[9]

It would be incomplete to suggest that mainstream voluntary organisations are not beginning to share these assumptions or not acknowledging contributions from their Black counterparts at all. It would also be immature to conclude that White voluntary organisations are not questioning the effects of personal and institutional racism in their managing, staffing and service structures. Well established organisations like British Agencies for Adoption and Fostering, Age Concern, Family Service Unit, Mind, Contact a Family, National Childrens Home and many others have been engaged in formulating race equality policies and promoting anti-racist practices, and liaising with Black voluntary organisations. There is also a noticeable change in the attitude and perception of social services departments in relation to Black organisations, in their attempts to forming alliances with these organisations. Although these changes in attitudes and attempts are not without difficulties,[10] there is now greater opportunities for social workers to get involved in this process of change. This they can do by:

(a) informing themselves about Black voluntary organisations, local and national,

(b) acting as a personal resource,

(c) making reference to Black organisation/s as a matter of practice, instead of making reference to white organisations as a rule,

(d) checking how prepared white organisations are in meeting the racial and cultural needs of their Black client/s, when references to white organisations are made,

(e) using the expertise of Black voluntary organisations not just to empower Black client/s, but in a way that obliterates any possibilities of exploiting them as 'dumping grounds',

(f) learning from these organisations about how to work within the framework of a 'holistic' approach and incorporate this approach in social work assessment and intervention,

(g) forming partnership with Black organisation/s in gaining resources and support from their own and other agencies, and

(h) establishing a trusting relationship with Black organisation/s.

Participation of voluntary organisations is not a new concept in social work. Report after report, recommendations after recommendations have kept this agenda going in social work scene. In the wake of the Wagner Report[11] and the White Paper in Community Care,[12] social work profession has perhaps never been so pushed to the voluntary sector. The role of the voluntary sector in providing welfare services, whether as charitable trusts or private enterprises, is bound to expand in the nineties. Whatever the speculations and debates on the pros and cons of these developments are, social workers have moral and professional obligations to ascertain that their involvements with voluntary sector is not 'all White' and their cooperation with Black voluntary sector is not 'mere tokens'.

Black Workers as a Resource for Change

There seems to exist a notion that Black workers' presence in social services and other related agencies is fairly recent. Yet, Black faces have not been that invisible in these agencies for some years. For example, there have not been that much shortage of Black cleaners, kitchen assistants and other manual workers or even clerical and administrative staff in welfare agencies, both in urban and rural settings. It is likely that these Black workers' invisibility has not been so much due to their absence, but because of their employment status within these agencies. I mention this specifically because most of the debates and arguments about recruiting more 'Black workers to meet the needs of Black clients' have somehow ignored this Black 'manual and non-professional' presence, who are workers as well. So, it seems that when we refer to Black workers in caring services, we mean Black 'professionals'. Whether one supports this distinction or not, I make this distinction for the purpose of this section for two reasons.

Firstly, although growing in numbers, there is still a case and will be for some time to come, for advancing the recruitment of Black social workers, Black managers and other Black professionals in caring agencies, if services are to be caring for Black communities. So the issue is not just about recruiting Black workers per se, but about increasing the number of Black professionals at all levels of service agencies. Secondly, till such time as when our institutions are able to break down the class barriers as professional hierarchy, Black professionals, to be effective as resource agents for change, have not much choice but to claim their professionalism. This they need to do on their own terms and conditions, which may mean redefining professionalism, that encapsulates the ideology of solidarity with all workers. Black professionalism and Black workers' solidarity are not in conflict. On the contrary, given the acknowledgement and recognition of their different and diverse attributions, they can radicalise working relationships in their agencies.

Reference to Black workers in this section is made within the context of Black professionals. Continuing reference to Black professionals as Black workers is based on a commonly shared ideology of most Black professionals, who prefer to call themselves 'Black workers'.

Manning (1979, 1981), in commenting on the response of social services to overcome their 'inadequacies' in relation to 'meeting the needs of black clients', expressed his concern about 'unclear definition' of Black workers' roles. Although he saw the potential of Black workers' existence as "important consequence for the black community who have long been arguing that the self-image of black children is impaired by the way in which black people in a classist society have been stereotyped" and as help for "black young people to improve both their self-image and their aspirations", he had some genuine fears as well. He feared that, "It would be an easy option to see black workers as working only with black clients", which would "fall easily into a dangerous trap set by precedents in British society which continue to treat black people as '*the problem*'". He also suspected that Black social workers could be "used by white social workers as an excuse to abdicate their responsibility for black clients". It is perhaps a great shame that Manning's concerns and fears were not unfounded. Reports and findings[14, 15, 16, 17, 18] have repeatedly substantiated these concerns and fears. In addition to taking on the burden of being perceived as part of the 'Black problem' and 'White abdication', Black social workers face prejudice in all shapes and forms – 'organisational prejudice', prejudice from white social workers and clients;[19] and their painful experiences are not spared even in an 'anti-racist' climate.[20] To sum up Black workers, even as professionals, are not exempted from racism. To this end they share the experiences of their co-black workers and clients. Despite all these, Black workers in caring professions have made meritorious contributions to social work profession. They can be a redeeming feature in empowering social work. They can be a prime resource for social work change. The following checklist aims to raise some questions that require positive answers, which in turn can outdistance opportunities for affirming Black workers as a resource for change:

1. Do you choose to see your Black colleagues as 'professionals' only or as 'Black professionals'? Make a list of advantages of your choices in relation to empowerment and change.

2. Do you think Black workers should be working with Black clients only or with both Black and White clients? List your perception of advantages and disadvantages of working with Black clients and/or white clients.

3. Do you believe that all/most Black workers should have 'cultural training' before/during their work with White clients? Justify your belief.

4. Do you believe that all/most White workers should have 'cultural training' before/during their work with Black clients? Justify your belief.

5. Have you done any joint work with your Black colleagues? What have you gained/learned from joint work?

6. Have you activiely sought advice/guidance from your Black colleagues? How have you benefitted from their advice/guidance?

7. Do you seek Black workers' advice/guidance only in relation to Black clients and/or 'race' issues? List your reasons for doing so. Also ask yourself why do you not consider seeking Black workers' advice/guidance on issues other than 'Black' or 'race'.

8. Do you tend to leave it to your Black colleagues to raise 'race' issues or matters related to Black clients in your workplace? If yes, clarify your reasons or motives. If no, make an inventory of when, where and how you raise these issues.

9. How do you support your Black colleagues? Are the terms and conditions of support decided by you? Black workers? Mutually agreed?

10. How do you cope with challenges and confrontations from your Black colleagues (and others)? Do you become defensive? Offensive? More guilt ridden? Positive? Make a note of your reactions.

11. How do you influence your co-workers (managers and supervisors as well) in relation to Black and 'race' issues? For? Against? How many supporters have you on your side as a result of your influence? How do you maintain this support?

12. Do you find it a must that whenever Black and 'race' issues are discussed by your Black co-workers, other equal opportunities issues such as sexism, disability, sexual orientation etc., are discussed as well? If you do, how do you ensure that Black and 'race' issues are not diffused or other issues take account of racism as well.

13. Finally, keep a progressive record of your own personal steps that you have taken, either in your workplace and/or elsewhere, in empowering Black workers as a resource for change.

Anti-Racist White Workers as a Resource for Change

"I am the only person in the whole department that talks about the needs of ethnic minorities."

"I get so frustrated . . . when I start talking I can feel people thinking 'here he goes, let him have his piece and we will carry on as usual' . . . yet anything to do with race I am supposed to be the person as long as I keep quiet and speak only when I am asked."

"I am not trusted by my white colleagues . . . they hide things from me . . . they think I will tell my Black friends."

"Because I am white, people say most racist things in front of me that they would not dare mention in front of blacks . . . I cringe . . . of course I become very angry . . . they say I am over reacting."

(Comments made by White professionals)

In a society, where policy makers are nearly all white, institutions are managed and serviced by mainly white people, practices are shaped by dominant white values and norms, achieving change for an equal society is going to remain an unreal dream without White workers joining the fight for equality and justice. Although few and far in between, it is most heartening to witness the progression of anti-racist White workers voicing their protest against racism and acting as change agents for race equality. It is vital that social work profession nurtures this progression and makes more headway with this progression. Most of the aforementioned 13 points checklist applies to anti-racist white workers as well, as long as they are adapted to fit the White experience, which by definition will be different to Black experience.

My selection of six areas of resources for change is by no means exhaustive. There are many other resources for change which are equally important for changing social work policy and practice to anti-racist social work empowerment. Political will and commitment, management determination and support, reallocation and redistribution of resources, anti-racist policy, legislative framework, organisational structures and procedures, non-racist social work education and training, all these are fundamental resources for change. It is not unknown how anti-racist initiatives face difficulties and experience frustration in a climate where these fundamental resources are not mobilised. However, it is also not unknown how individual initiatives and perseverence can mobilise resources for change and influence the process of change for making social work responsive, effective and equitable to its receivers, no matter what the constraints are. To undermine or ignore the capacity of individual professionals in influencing and changing their profession for better, is to dismiss professional aspirations and satisfactions. More importantly, if there is an argument that without political will or management commitment, social workers can never fulfill their anti-racist aspirations and expectations, then it must also follow that social workers are falling short of fulfilling their professional responsibility and credibility in relation to their Black clients. The six areas of resources for change that have been selected in this section, although have implications for policy makers and managers, are specifically targetted to address social workers' personal responsibility for bettering social work profession and making it credible to Black communities.

References

1. Seebohm – *Report of the Committee on Local Authority and Allied personal Services* – HMSO 1968.

2. Rt. Hon. G. Thomas – Address of Welcome – *Participation in community Life* – Report of the Seventh British National Conference on Social Welfare – Published by the National Council of Social Service, 1970.

3. U. Prashar and S. Nicholas – *Routes or Roadblocks? Consulting minority communities in London boroughs* – the Runnymede Trust, 1986.
4. Commission For Racial Equality – *Racial Equality In Social Services Departments* – A survey of Equal Opportunity Policies – 1989.
5. *Caring for People – Community Care In The Next Decade And Beyond – Caring for The 1990s* – White Paper HMSO 1982.
6. *Children Act 1989* – HMSO 1980.
7. J. M. Martin & E. P. Martin – *The Helping Tradition In The Black Family And Community* – National Association of Social Workers, Inc. 1985.
8. *Submission to the White Paper in Community Care by the Race Equality Unit* – personal social services (National Institute For Social Work) – see Appendix 1.
9. B. Ahmad – *When sharing assumptions can pave the way to partnerships* – Social Work Today, 8.12.1989.
10. ibid no. 9.
11. *Residential Care – A Positive Choice – Report of the Independent review of Residential Care* – National Institute For social Work, HMSO 1988.
12. ibid no. 5.
13. B. Manning – *The Black Social Work's Role* – Social work Today (20.2.79) and *Social & Community Work In A Multi-Racial Society*, Eds. Cheetham, James, Loney, Mayor and Prescott, Open University – Harper & Row 1981.
14. N. Connelly – *Social services Departments and Race*: A discussion paper. Policy Stuies Institute (PSI) 1985 and Care in the Multiracial community, PSI 1988.
15. B. Rooney – *Racism and Resistance to change* – A Study of the Black Social Workers Project – Liverpool Social Services Department – University of Liverpool 1987.
16. D. Divine – *A Study on Probation Service* – 1989. Unpublished.
17. *Networking for Change* – A Report by North West Region Black Workers Group in Social Services, 1989, awaiting publication.
18. J. Durrant – Moving forward in a multiracial society – Community Care 7.12.1989.
19. V. Liverpool – *The Dilemmas and Contribution of Black Social workers – Social work and ethnicity* Ed. Cheetham – Allan & Unwin 1982.
20. B. Ahmad – *Black Pain, White Hurt* – Social Work Today 14.12.1989.

Chapter 4
Social Work and Legislation

Social work policy and practice does not usually relate its statutory and legal duties to Race Relations Act 1976 (RRA 1976). Yet RRA 1976 has significant implications for social work. This chapter identifies some of the main implications. It also makes a brief reference to those sections of Community Care (Caring for People – Community Care In The Next Decade and Beyond – Caring for 1990s) and Children Act 1989 that specifically refer to Black and Minority Ethnic Communities, families and children.

Social Work and Race Relations Act 1976

The Race Relations Act (RRA) 1976, which applies to Britain (not Northern Ireland), makes racial discrimination unlawful in employment, training and related matters, in education, in the provision of goods, facilities and services, and in the management of premises.

As the functions of local authorities cover all the above areas, and social services departments are part of local authority structures, fulfillment of legal requirements of the RRA Act 1976 is a responsibility of all social services departments. Within the framework of the legal provision, RR Act 1976 imposes specific obligations and duties on local authorities and consequently on social services as well.

One of the essential prerequisites of meaningful and effective application of RR Act 1976 is a clear understanding of the justification, the spirit, and the rationale prompting the Act.

The justification for RR Act, which first came into force in 1968, amended in 1973 and further amended in 1976, was based on an acknowledgement that racial discrimination existed and that legal provision was needed to remedy the situation. It was also a recognition of injustice perpetuated by racial discrimination and Central Government's response to prolonged campaigning and incidents of civil unrest during the 50's and 60's.

The spirit of the RR Act 1976 is best expressed in the White Paper preceding the RR Act 1976, which took account of the past discrimination and its accumulative effects and realised that – "Too literal a meaning of non-discrimination would in fact impede equal opportunity as it would exclude special training, encouragement, etc . . . " In other words the RR Act 1976 is not just to remedy racial discrimination but also to achieve race equality.

The main rationale prompting the RR Act from 1968 onwards must be, if there was no racial discrimination, there would have been no need for a legal provision. If the presupposition of the RR Act/s is the existence of racial discrimination, then there must exist those who are Discriminators and those who are being Discriminated.

The objective of the RR Act can only be achieved when a legal remedy is able to impose sanctions against the Discriminator and confer rights to the Discriminated.

Section 71 imposes a duty on local authorities to:
(a) eliminate racial discrimination
(b) promote equality of opportunity and good race relations

Since the main functions of local authorities and social services is to provide services to its communities, and in order to provide services it employs persons, and in order to equip persons delivering services it provides education and training for acquiring relevant skills and knowledge, the application of Section 71 relate to two areas – Service Delivery and Employment.

The following Sections of RR Act 1976 enable social services to fulfil their legal obligation of Section 71.

Section 1 (1A) defines direct racial discriminations as arising where a person treats another person less favourably on racial grounds than s/he treats, or would treat, someone else.

Section 1 (1b) defines indirect discriminations as treatment which may be described as equal in a formal sense as between different racial groups but discriminatory in its effect on one particular racial group.

For social services this section has crucial implications, as manifestations of Indirect Discrimination is rife in institutional procedures, customs and practices, even though they are not designed to be intentionally discriminatory, but by default they are and in effect they are contibutory factors to Institutional Racism. For example, lack of appropriate residential/day care and domicillary care for Black elders and criteria for providing these services leave many of them without provisions such as meals on wheels, Luncheon clubs, day centres etc.

Section 20 applies to those who are concerned with the provision of goods, facilities and services to the public or section of the public. If for example social services as provider of services discriminates by refusing or deliberately omitting service provisions, then it is in breach of RR Act 1976. The legal duties under Section 20 go beyond refusal and omission and extend to the discrimination in quality of services and the manner in which or the terms on which they are provided. An appropriate example of quality of services and the manner in which the services are provided is the absence of linguistic knowledge and skills of social work professionals, who canot speak the language of their clients. Incidents of social workers making wrong assessment and decisions about their Black clients with discriminatory consequences are not uncommon in social work practices.

Section 40 (1) makes it unlawful to discriminate in the way in which access to benefits, facilities or services are afforded and facilitated. For Social Workers, who are often the gatekeepers of services, this section has major implications. In most instances, Black clients' access to social services facilities and benefits are dependant on how and to what extent social workers ensure their access to appropriate services. This includes information about available services as well.

Section 4 (1) lays down the legal requirements in terms of recruitment and makes it unlawful if the arrangements for deciding the offer of employment, the terms offered are discriminatory and if employment is refused and deliberately omitted.

Section 4 (a) is breached if discrimination occurs in the way of affording access to opportunities for promotion, transfer or training or to any other benefits, facilities or services or if access is refused or deliberately omitted.

Section 5 permits employers to take positive action in recruiting for a job or in providing opportunities for promotion, transfer or training for a job where being a particular racial group is a genuine occupational qualification for the job. The most relevant criteria for social services in determining if being of a particular racial group is a genuine occupation qualification is "the job-holder provides persons of the racial group in question with personal services promoting their welfare and those services can most effectively be provided by a person of the same racial group."

Section 35 allows for "acts done to enable the special needs of particular racial groups to be met as regards education, training or welfare or ancillary benefits". Benefits can be restricted, or allocated first, if it can be shown that members of that racial group have a special need which is met by such acts.

Section 38 of the Act allows employers to take positive action in providing access to facilities for training for that work to employees of a particular racial group only, and also in encouraging members of that racial group to take advantage of opportunities for doing work.

Section 39 legalises placement of advertisement indicating the intention of positive action.

Section 47 provides that the Commission for Racial Equality may issue codes of practice containing guidance on:

(a) The elimination of discrimination in the field of employment.
(b) The promotion of equality of opportunity in that field between persons of different racial groups.

The Code of Practice, which came into effect on 1 April 1984, gives detailed guidelines on many aspects of employment, e.g. criteria for selection, advertising, conditions of work, grievance procedure, etc. It also gives guidelines on the adoption and monitoring of an Equal Opportunity Policy in order to ensure that the provisions of the Act are put into practice.

The Code does not impose any legal obligations itself, nor is it an authoritative statement of the law – that can only be provided by the courts and tribunals. If, however, its recommendations are not observed this may result in breaches of the law. Moreover, its provisions are admissible in evidence in any proceedings under the RRA 1976 before an Industrial Tribunal. Therefore, although the Code is in itself not a statement of the law its provisions are binding in that they need to be followed if local authorities are to fulfil their legal obligation to eliminate racial discrimination and promote equality of opportunity and good race relations.

The provision of RR Act 1976 in itself is not a guarantee for eliminating racial discrimination and promoting equality of opportunity and good race relations in social services departments. The effective use of the act depends on the commitment social workers have in implementing the RR Act's legal requirements. In doing so, social workers not only may find some of the practical measures for pursuing Race Equality policies and practices, but may indeed set precedence for their local authorities and other services.

The Children Act 1989

The central and continuing theme throughout the Children Act 1989 is the Welfare of the Child and promotion of the child's welfare, child protection and safeguarding the child's interest are paramount considerations of the Act.

Within the central theme and paramount considerations, Social workers have legal obligations to promote the welfar of the Black child, protect the Black child and safeguard his/her interest as well as all other children. Thus all sections of Children Act have implications for Black Children, not just the specific sections referring to race, religion and ethnic origin. It must then follow that if social workers are to fulfil all their promoting and protecting duties, then their practice with Black children has to be non-racist and non-discriminatory. Failing this the Black child's welfare may not be safeguarded, nor can his/her interest be protected.

Specific reference to a child's religious background or persuasion has been part of Child Care law for some years. The Children Act 1989 is the first legislation regarding children that includes not just religion but three other important factors as well – a child's racial origin, ethnic and linguistic background. This has major implications for social workers and authorities, as it will be unlawful to ignore the race, culture, language and religion of children who are looked after by the statutory and voluntary institutions.

Section 22(5) (c) of The Children Act 1989 clearly requires local authorities and voluntary organisations to give due considerations to "the child's religious persuasion, racial origin and cultural and linguistic background". In practical terms these considerations mean ensuring proper consultation with parents and other adults who are important to the child, seeking their views, opinions and feelings, taking account of the child's views, experience and feelings in the decision making process. It also implies making appropriate arrangements for the child on the basis of due considerations given on the child's race, culture, language and religion.

As in section 22 (5), other sections of the Act state the same requirement, such as in Section 61 (3) (c) regarding Voluntary Homes and Voluntary Organisations, Section 64 (3) (c) regarding Registered Children's Homes. Under section 74 (6) of the ACT, local authorities are duty bound to "have regard to the child's religious persuasion, racial origin and cultural and linguistic background" and ensure that the childminders and other Day Care providers meet these needs of the child. This section allows local authorities to cancel the registration of childminders and other day care providers if their care is "seriously inadequate" in meeting the racial, cultural, linguistic and religious needs of the child. According to this section, racist attitude of day carers should be regarded as one of the reasons for cancelling their registrations.

One of the arguments that held the attention of the Parliamentary debates on the Children Act 1989 was a concern about services not reflecting the ethnic mix of local communities. Introduction of Paragraph 11 in Schedule 2 was in response to this concern which makes it a "Duty to consider racial groups to which children in need belong". This requirement implies that local authorities should have day and foster carers from all sections of their communities. Active implementation of this requirement may indeed build up a valuable resource of Black Foster parent and carers and end the tiring excuses for not promoting "same race placement policy".

Under Section 17 (1) (a) and (b), the local authorities have duty to "safeguard and promote the welfare of children within their areas" and "promote the upbringing of such children (who are in need) by their families". So far, the experience of Black children in need has been quite the opposite. Often they are removed from their areas, families and communities. This must raise legal as well as professional concern. Social worekrs should be able to make positive use of the Children Act, which strongly advocates for maintaining children in their own families and includes members of "extended" families for this purpose. In terms of contact or residence orders, family members such as aunt, uncle, grandparent or any other interested adult can apply to the court for parental responsibility. Promotion and effective use of this legal provision may indeed see a considerable reduction of Black children being removed from their families and communities and the inevitable pain and sufferings experienced by so many Black aunts, uncles, grandparents and relatives. It is apposite to point out here that the new

Act encourages the social workers to place children within their own family network. Should it be the case that social workers do not do so, relatives of the children will be able to apply for a residence order with the permission of the court and if granted, care order will be automatically discharged. Section 8 of the Act provides a flexible range of new orders that have much potential for ethnically sensitive responses to Black children and their families.

With reference to the "Welfare of the Child", section 1 (3) (d) states that the "court shall have regard in particular to his (child's) age, sex, background and any characteristics of his which the court considers relevant". This section has particular importance for Section 7 (1) (a) and (b) on welfare reports, which authorises a court to ask for report from probation officer or an officer or such other person arranged by a local authority to report to the court on such matters relating to the welfare of that child. Apart from regarding a child's ethnicity and racial experience as one such matter of welfare of a Black child, social workers can apply this section as an advocating aid to influence the court in ensuring due consideration of Black children's racial and cultural needs.

Although the Children Act 1989 has legal provisions for responding to the racial, cultural, religious and linguistic needs of Black and Minority children, it's interpretation and application will depend on how committed social workers are to make maximum use of the Act. For example, they may have different definitions and criteria of "due consideration" as opposed to "paramount consideration" of the Act. Whatever their definitions are and however varied the criteria for "due consideration" may be, the fact is that the welfare of the Black children can neither be promoted nor be protected fully without giving paramount consideration to their racial and cultural background.

The White Paper on community Care

Section 2.9 of the White Paper refers to "People from Ethnic Minorities." It States –

"The Government recognises that people from different cultural backgrounds may have particular care needs and problems. Minority communities may have different concepts of community care and it is important that service providers are sensitive to these variations. Good community care will take account of the circumstances of minority communities and will be planned in consultation with them."

It is important to realise that Black people's needs of community care is not just confined to section 2.9. All sections of the White Paper have implication for Black communities and their organisations. In 1989, the Race Equality Unit – Personal Social Services (National Institute for Social Work) made its submission to the White Paper. The submission pointed out the main implications and made appropriate recommendations.

The submission also provides a framework for developing community care for Black people. Appendix I includes the submission.

Conclusion

"Racism is an inherent part of this society and in social services is a fundamental barrier to the development of policies and practices that allow the effective provision of services to Black and Minority Ethnic families and communities. Racism permeates social service structures and all aspects of service delivery with harmful and damaging effects. Racism results in denying Black people their welfare and rights and leaves White people with a distorted view of the reality." (A statement of belief – Race Equality Unit – Personal Social Services – National Institute For Social Work)

Social workers and allied professionals are part of social services (and related agencies) structures. They are the gate keepers of caring services, as well as providers of social services. As gate-keepers, they can, if they wish to, remove the barriers of racism and let anti-racist social work enter in their social services structures. As service providers, they can, if they are willing, reverse the denial of welfare and rights of Black families they are working for and change the face of their social work practice to an empowering, non-racist social practice.

The making of anti-racist social work practice is not going to happen if social workers remain complacent and pretend that all is well with social work for Black people, or really not too bad. Nor is it going to happen, if social workers keep on waiting for their political masters and managers to hold their hands in paving their path for anti-racist social work. As it is true that race-equality in social work should be a concern for all, it is also a fact that without social work action for equality, political statements of intent and management policies for equal opportunities, can be reduced to mere rhetorics and gestures.

Social work action is dependent on social workers and allied professions—the gate-keepers and providers of direct services. They have inherent power in their gate-keeping and provider roles in addition to their professional power invested in their social work role. Professional power that can either intervene and control clients with social problems or use the power more for protection and prevention; that can either assess real needs of clients or abuse the professional power by distorting their needs; that can either respond to the real needs of clients and explore every possible alternatives and options to meet those needs or respond in a manner which has little relevance to clients' real needs; and professional power that can either be used to protect professional interests above the interest of clients or be directed to empower clients. The first three chapters give many examples of how social workers can make best use of their professional status and power to emancipate their practice with Black families and act as agents for social work empowerment. Checklists, guidelines, comments and suggestions in each chapter provide much scope for social workers to develop further and work on their personal code of anti-racist practice, that is adaptable and applicable in their own workplace experiences and circumstances. Developing and working on anti-racist code of social work practice is not just about adaptability and applicability, it is also about challenging those aspects of social work practice that have racist effect and outcome and changing them. For this reason, throughout the book, references to challenge and change, protest and propose, have aimed to strike a balance between anti-racist aspirations and possible practical actions, between anti-racist expectations and achievable targets for equality.

Even the most ardent advocates of equality and justice would not place the whole burden of eradicating racism and racial discrimination from British society on social workers. Changes in Black people's political, economical and social inequality are big issues that can occur when there is a combined force from various sections that is energised by new direction and action, that is guided by conviction and commitment and that is enriched by shared experience and knowledge. Social workers are not expected to solve Britain's 'race' problem. But they have a duty to resolve racism in their own profession, to say the least. They have an obligation to rid social work of oppressive practices. Failing to do so, social work will continue to be one of the most controlling devices for keeping Black families, in need of welfare services, down and under. Social workers hold the reins of real empowerment of Black families and clients. The questions then are—When will each and every social worker realise that they are at the interface of social work change for racial equality? How are they going to transfer this realisation in their day to day anti-racist practice? What are their empowerment strategies for Black families and clients? Are they to hold tight the strings of social work power and control over Black families? Or are they to let go of disempowering holds and join hands with Black families, in their fight against racism and fight for empowerment?

Appendix
Race Equality Unit, National Institute for Social Work Submission to The White Paper on Community Care

Black and Minority Ethnic communities are in urgent need of community care services. A serious imbalance exists at present – existing statutory services in large measure fail to take into account the needs of people in Black and Minority Ethnic Communities. Services are not accessible or appropriate, information is not available or sensitively delivered to Black users and carers, assessments fail to take cultural factors into account. The allocation of resources for community care is not equitable across the different communities. Black and Minority Ethnic communities suffer from a services and resources deficit which urgently needs to be redressed.

Many community care needs of Black and Minority Ethnic people are met at present by voluntary and community organisations. Typically, such Black and Minority Ethnic organisations are seriously under-resourced, and are trying to do a crucial job under immense pressure, with little support. In some areas, Black and Minority Ethnic communities are too small or sparsely scattered to sustain even that safety-net.

The White Paper on Community Care, in laying down a framework for the future, should make a point of ensuring that the needs of Black and Minority Ethnic users, carers and communities are fully taken into account by those responsible for community care, that full and meaningful consultation takes place and that positive action is taken to redress current imbalances.

We recommend that:

Recommendation 1
The White Paper makes reference to equal opportunities and recognises the need for anti-racist and anti-discriminatory strategies for providing services for Black and Minority Ethnic populations.

Justification
To redress the past imbalance of unequal resources available or accessible to Black and Minority Ethnic Communities and ensure their needs are being met effectively.

Recommendation 2
The White Paper clarifies the statutory duties and legal responsibilities that community care planners, service providers and co-ordinates and assessors have for providing appropriate and adequate services to Black and Minority Ethnic populations.

Justification
To rectify omission and/or marginalisation of Black and Minority Ethnic communities' needs and establish multi-ethnic community care services in mainstream agencies as an integral part of community care planning.

Recommendation 3
The White Paper acknowledges the diverse and differing needs of Black and Minority Ethnic populations as an essential pre-requisite for providing different community care services 'as opposed to the "same" approach adopted for White and Majority Ethnic populations.

Justification
To eliminate myths and cultural stereotypes and work against "colour blind" approach.

Recommendation 4
The White Paper validates the contributions made by Black and Minority Ethnic Voluntary Organisations in providing community care services and strongly recommends support and resources from mainstream authorities and agencies to these organisations.

Justification
To ensure appropriate use of community resources and benefit from the innovative experience of Black and Minority Ethnic Voluntary Organisations, that have well established valuable holistic approaches in community care.

Recommendation 5
The White Paper recommends positive action to negotiate with and award contracts to Black and Minority Ethnic Voluntary Organisations and groups.

Justification
To acknowledge to the fact that White organisations have a higher profile with local authorities than Black organisations and as such have a headstart.

Recommendation 6
The White Paper gives explicit guidance to local authorities about the allocation of budgets (care element of social security budget) for private

and voluntary residential care establishments catering for Black and Minority Ethnic Communities.

Justification
There has been little or no benefit to the residential care of Black and Minority Ethnic communities, inspite of the rapid rise in the social security budget. Consequently, there is a large reservoir of unmet needs in these communities which merit attention and action.

Recommendation 7
The White Paper makes it a requirement for all community care planners, providers, co-ordinators and assessors to consult Black and Minority Ethnic users, carers and service providing groups in planning and resourcing community care services and to provide information about services to Black and Minority Ethnic communities.

Justification
To enable mainstream authorities and agencies to gain knowledge and information about community care needs of Black and Minority Ethnic users, carers and service providing groups and promote meaningful participation of Black and Minority Ethnic communities in the decision-making process.

Recommendation 8
The White Paper makes it mandatory for statutory agencies to assess in their local profiles the demographic construction of Black and Minority Ethnic communities in their areas and their present services access.

Justification
To identify the implications of community care planning for Black communities, including allocation of resources, service delivery and ethnic composition of staff.

Recommendation 9
The White Paper makes specific recommendations for recruiting Black and Minority Ethnic staff and anti-racist training for all staff responsible for designing and delivering packages of care.

Justification
To enhance the quality of community care for Black and Minority Ethnic communities and promote ethnically sensitive packages of care.

Recommendation 10
The White Paper gives special attention to the criteria for assessment to be undertaken by people with appropriate awareness, understanding and knowledge of the needs of community care of Black and Minority Ethnic communities and includes right of appeal.

Justification
To ensure community care services are accessible and available to Black and Minority Ethnic users and carers.

Recommendation 11
The White Paper priorities both quantiative and qualitative monitoring of all community care services for Black and Minority Ethnic communities as essential part of community care policies and practices, and recommends representation of Black and Minority Ethnic users, carers and service providing groups in the monitoring process.

Justification
To make services accountable to Black and Minority Ethnic communities in needs of community care and to evaluate quantitative and qualitative aspects of services provided (or not), including performance of service planners and providers.

Recommendation 12
The White Paper recognises the need for National guidance for the quantity and quality of community care services that are able to respond to the needs of Black and Minority Ethnic users and carers. To this end, the White Paper recommends the establishment of a Working Group with Black and Minority Ethnic involvement and representation.

Justification
To ensure that community care services for Black and Minority Ethnic communities are comprehensive, consistent and anti-discriminatory.

This paper was prepared by the Race Equality Unit at the National Institute for Social Work. It follows two working groups: the Griffiths Task Force of officers from local authorities and a joint meeting, with the Community Care Project of the National Council for Voluntary Organisations, of Black and Minority Ethnic Voluntary organisations.

September 1989.

INDEX